THE ISLAND OF THE FOUR Ps

A MODERN FABLE ABOUT PREPARING FOR YOUR FUTURE

ALSO BY ED HAJIM

On the Road Less Traveled:
An Unlikely Journey from the Orphanage to the Boardroom

THE ISLAND OF THE FOUR Ps

A MODERN FABLE ABOUT PREPARING FOR YOUR FUTURE

ED HAJIM

with Merrill Meadow

Illustrated by GABRIELA LEAL
Edited by GLENN PLASKIN

Skyhorse Publishing

Skyhorse Publishing books may be purchased in bulk at special discounts for sales promotion, corporate gifts, fund-raising, or educational purposes. Special editions can also be created to specifications. For details, contact the Special Sales Department, Skyhorse Publishing, 307 West 36th Street, 11th Floor, New York, NY 10018 or info@skyhorsepublishing.com.

Skyhorse and Skyhorse Publishing are registered trademarks of Skyhorse Publishing, Inc., a Delaware corporation.

Visit our website at www.skyhorsepublishing.com.

10 9 8 7 6 5 4 3 2 1

Library of Congress Cataloging-in-Publication Data is available on file.

Cover design by David Ter-Avanesyan
Cover illustration credit: Gabriela Leal

Interior illustrations: Gabriela Leal

Print ISBN: 978-1-5107-7617-3
Ebook ISBN: 978-1-5107-7618-0

Printed in China

For my family—*my wonderful wife, Barbara; our three children, G.B., Brad, and Corey; their spouses, Karen, Marthe, and Jim; and our grandchildren, Ra'am, Noam, Luka, Leo, Emma, Sammy, Eddie, and Oscar.*

To the University of Rochester and Harvard Business School—*for giving me the education that changed my life.*

To the United States of America—*for giving me the opportunity to realize my dreams.*

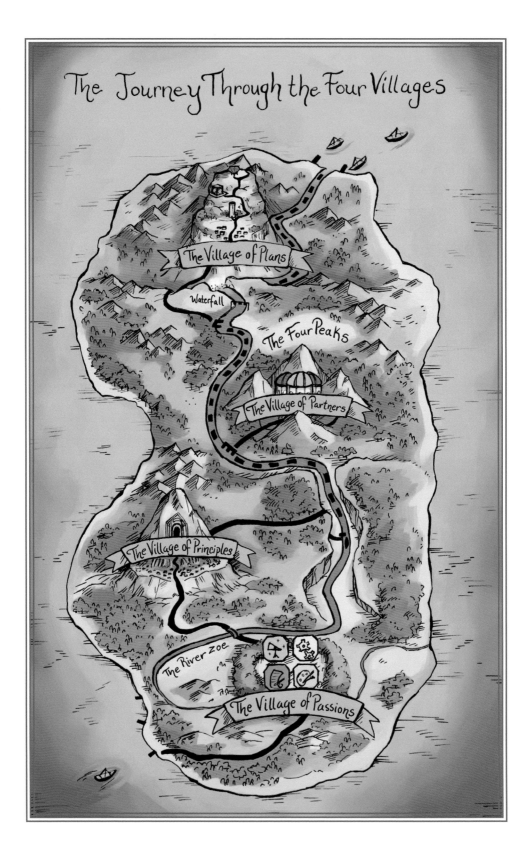

CONTENTS

ACKNOWLEDGMENTS

T he *Island of the Four Ps* is about the decisions we make and *how* we make them. The decision-making touchstones I use, the Four Ps, have guided me for a lifetime. If there's anything certain in this world, it's that we face innumerable forks in the road, decision points that affect our destinies. As you begin your journey, I hope the story in the pages that follow will provide direction and inspiration.

I could not have written *The Island of the Four Ps* without the help and encouragement of my family and colleagues, who provided me with unconditional love and support.

First and foremost, no words can fully describe my wonderful wife of fifty-seven years, Barbara. She is the heart and soul of our family—my best friend, my life partner, the most attentive mother and grandmother imaginable, and the true source of my happiness. Our partnership is my most precious asset. Barbara not only put up with me as I was writing this book, she also stood ready to help with the writing and editing, providing invaluable feedback.

I must also thank our three children, G.B., Brad, and Corey. Corey also wrote some of the material about my early years.

Many of the ideas here were inspired by brilliant books that helped shape my perspective on life. These include: *The Seasons of a Man's Life* by Daniel J. Levinson; *The Pyramid of Success* by John Wooden; and *Three Rules for Living a Good Life* by Lou Holtz. Special thanks must also go to Howard Stevenson, the author of *Just Enough: Tools for Creating Success in Your Work and Life.* His book is filled with incredible wisdom, some of which I've incorporated into this book.

As far as the production of this book is concerned, I must recognize my collaborator, Merrill Meadow, who contributed much of the writing. Over a period of two years, he traveled from Boston to New York City to interview me as we worked on the book. Although the concept of the Four Ps is mine, it is Merrill's creativity that captured what I was trying to convey. Most of the characters and village descriptions come from his imagination. So without his partnership, *The Island of the Four Ps* might never have seen the light of day.

I also want to thank our brilliant illustrator, Gabriela Leal, who re-created the essence of our story in pictures.

The magical travels of our main characters are brought to life by her artistic renderings. Her ability to quickly understand the environment I saw in my mind's eye was nothing short of amazing.

To put the finishing touches on the book, I turned to *New York Times* bestselling author Glenn Plaskin, who was my partner on my first book, *On the Road Less Traveled*. His insightful editing was crucial in getting the manuscript ready for the publisher. His knowledge of the first book helped a great deal in fitting the two books together. And his ability to understand how to correctly convey an idea or position was essential to this process. Thanks, Glenn!

I also want to thank Glenn's brilliant copyeditor, Barbara Clark, who reviewed the final manuscript with care.

A special note of thanks to my longtime book designer Michelle Manley, who kindly consulted on this project, offering astute enhancements to both the interior and exterior of the book.

Next, I wish to thank literary legend Tony Lyons, the president and founder of Skyhorse Publishing, who has believed in me from the start. Skyhorse has been meticulous in creating the best platform possible, and I am grateful for it.

My thanks, of course, also go to Skyhorse senior editor Julie Ganz, who guided the book to publication with calm expertise. Other able members of the Skyhorse team include jacket designer David Ter-Avanesyan and senior production editor Kirsten Dalley. I am grateful for their attention and hard work.

Equally important, I must thank my incredible publicist, the brilliant Meryl Moss, and her associate Tracy Goldblatt. Meryl and I have become true partners. She produced the rollout campaign for my first book, *On the Road Less Traveled*, and has done a wonderful job in launching this book.

One additional note: I first developed the concept of the Four Ps while I was writing a commencement speech for graduating classes at the University of Rochester, where I was chairman of the board of trustees at the time. Thanks are due to the many members of the university's staff and administration for their input and support as I developed the themes for the speech, which ultimately became the key concepts for this book.

I also want to thank the esteemed colleagues and friends who wrote generously kind testimonials for my first book. They include Dr. Dale V. Atkins, A. Charles Baillie, Bob Callahan, Robert L. Clark, Raj Echambadi, Renée Fleming, Barbara Hackman Franklin, Sol Gittleman, Wendi Heinzelman, Ralph Kuncl, Andrew Lippa, Ken Roman, Joel Seligman, and Mark Zupan.

Finally, I must thank the friends and colleagues who were kind enough to read *On the Road Less Traveled*. I appreciate their commenting so favorably about the Four Ps as they were set forth in that book's epilogue, further encouraging me to pursue the publication of *The Island of the Four Ps*.

L et's be frank: we live in unusual times.

The future "normal" is going to be very different from what most of us have experienced. It's going to be even more dynamic and perhaps less certain. We'll see enormous changes in our culture, our economy, and our day-to-day lives.

From the vantage point of 2023, some of those changes will be driven by our new understanding of what the word "pandemic" means. But the drivers of change will be far broader. In the next decade, digitization, artificial intelligence, and automation are going to fundamentally change what work, community, career, and success mean for most people. In fact, many of the jobs that American workers will perform in the 2030s haven't been invented yet. At the same time, the many effects of climate change will force us to consider new ways of interacting with the world around us and conducting our day-to-day lives.

How do you prepare yourself to deal with that kind of change? How do you learn to cope with the uncertainty and fear that often come with waves of change?

Here, in basic terms, is my answer: First, you learn *who* you are—what you believe, what motivates you, what scares you, and what will help you realize your full potential. Second, you learn to identify the good things about change. You eagerly ask, "What's next?" and seize the opportunities that come down the road. My purpose in this book is to help you take those two steps by applying the lessons I learned through my own scary and difficult personal experiences, which you'll read about in part 2. The instability I felt at that time had everything to do with my quest for a purpose in adulthood. Scary as my circumstance might have been, they ignited in me a desire to find my purpose and plan for the future I wanted.

That's why I wrote this book—so you can use my experience to help you navigate troubled waters. No matter what your profession or stage of life, there are moments when you will need direction—a compass that leads you to what's next. I've always depended on that in my career on Wall Street.

But as you'll see, *The Island of the Four Ps* is not a how-to business book. It is a think-about-it book in the form of a fable. As Tony Robbins has often said, people understand concepts and learn best when they are emotionally affected by a *story*, in this case a fable.

Why a fable? Why not just set out the key ideas and say, "Do it this way"? Because I don't believe there's only one way to deal with life transitions. And even if you accept my ideas wholly, there is no single right way to put them into action.

The Island of the Four Ps is a fable about the huge, scary challenge we all face: carving our path to success and happiness. It uses fiction to capture the truth of human experience—our striving and yearning, our courage, joys, and fears. So as you read, join along in the quest. Think about ways the fable might reflect your own life. Take a journey of the imagination and consider your day-to-day experience in a new light.

I hope you will find this book easy and entertaining to read. But as you'll see, there are life lessons built into the story. So don't just glide through it. Put a little energy into pondering the ideas it offers—accepting, modifying, or rejecting them as you think best. Read *The Island of the Four Ps* one chapter at a time, then answer the few questions I pose at the end of each one. Or read the book through from start to finish, then come back and answer the questions chapter by chapter.

You'll be rewarded for taking your time. I hope *The Island of the Four Ps* will prompt you to contemplate who you are and what you want in life. Ideally, it will spur you to action—helping you engage fully in life, pursue new experiences, and surf the waves of change.

PART I

The Fable

CHAPTER ONE

A QUEST BEGINS

A young man, Marketus, stood on the prow of a small boat. For several moments, he watched green tips of forested mountains rise slowly from the horizon. Then he called to the boat's captain and navigator. "Look! I think we're almost there."

The captain glanced ahead with a smile, pleased by the enthusiasm in the young voyager's voice. Turning to her partner, the navigator, she said, "It is an extraordinary view, isn't it?"

"Yes," the navigator replied, "and after all these years, I still remember the mix of emotions I felt when I first arrived. Excitement, energy, and a little fear."

"It feels good, helping this young adventurer begin his own quest," the captain said as Marketus joined them at the wheel. The three stood together and watched as the land appeared. First, a ridge of mountains surrounded by heavily forested hills. Then a thin ribbon of beach connecting forest and ocean.

Looking back over the distance they had crossed, Marketus saw many other boats spread across the waters behind them. Most carried families accompanying other young voyagers. But Marketus's sole companions were the captain and navigator. They'd recognized something special in him and generously offered to transport him to the Island of the Four Ps.

Marketus knew that the other young voyagers all came from a wide variety of backgrounds. And once they reached their destination, each would embark on an individual quest, at his or her own pace. This would not be some kind of race.

"Though your paths may cross," the navigator had said to Marketus, "you must undertake this quest independently. The lessons you learn must be your own."

"However, that doesn't mean you'll be alone," the captain noted. "We've arranged for someone to accompany you. His name is Archimedes."

Marketus asked, "Wasn't Archimedes the ancient Greek mathematician who invented ways to accomplish difficult things easily—like lifting heavy objects and pumping water from a deep well?"

"Exactly," the navigator replied. "Like his Greek namesake, our Archimedes will give you tools to make *your* work easier and more effective. But you must make the effort yourself."

———

An hour later, Marketus stood alone on a gently sloping beach, carrying only a backpack, a compass, and a book. The captain and navigator waved a last goodbye and backed their boat away from the shore. They knew that when they saw Marketus again he would be transformed: a little wiser, more mature, and more confident about his future.

Marketus felt a twinge of regret about this parting, but he also felt the exhilaration that comes with new-found freedom. For the first time in his life, he held his destiny in his own hands. He was ready to explore the uncharted territory before him.

The mountains rose from the beach in fits and starts: forested hills led to valleys, then higher hills eventually rose to form a range of peaks. The forests were deep, broken now and then by fields of wild grasses, broad lakes, and swiftly flowing rivers.

Marketus wondered if he was destined to climb those peaks. What might lie beyond them? More important, where should he begin? He scanned the tree line ahead for a clear starting point. But everything appeared dark and a little foreboding.

Then a man emerged from the trees. Dressed in simple clothes, he had a satchel slung across his shoulders. The man walked into the sunlight and stopped, basking in the warmth. He wore the broad smile of someone returning to a well-loved spot. After a moment, he turned and walked directly toward Marketus.

"Hello, Marketus. My name is Archimedes," he said.

"Hello," Marketus replied. "The captain and navigator told me to expect you." Then he asked, "Are you an inventor, too, like the other Archimedes?"

"Nowhere near as accomplished as he was, but I have invented this," Archimedes said, taking from his satchel a small item wrapped in cloth, which he handed to Marketus.

Unwrapping it, Marketus found an oblong metal object. Depending on how the light struck it, it looked to be made of copper, silver, or gold. It was flat on top except for four deep indentations set around a raised circle. Rounded on the bottom, it fit easily in his palm.

"It is a *tessares makhana*," Archimedes said. "In Greek, that means 'a machine of four elements.' But for simplicity, I just call it a Tessamark."

"What's it do?"

"At the moment, nothing. By the time we reach the other side of that mountain range, though, you will see what it can do. In fact, learning to use the Tessamark is key to your quest's success. For now, put it your pocket and keep it safe."

With that, he settled the satchel on his shoulder and gestured toward the trees. The two companions started walking.

At the tree line, Marketus paused to look back. Farther down the beach, a handful of boats were drawing away from land, each having deposited a lone voyager. "Will all those voyagers have a guide, too?" he asked.

"Unfortunately, no," Archimedes answered. "Many will wander about fruitlessly and miss out on the knowledge this land offers." Then he walked into the dense forest, and Marketus followed.

As they walked, they fell easily into conversation— about Marketus's life, his friends, the fact that he was an orphan, and his most memorable experiences. In the quiet moments in between, Marketus looked closely at the environment around them. From time to time, he used the compass to check their direction. But he soon realized it was purposeless. Although their first destination was, Archimedes said, due east of the beach, the winding trails hit all points of the compass. There were many intersecting and inviting paths, some of which they followed, some of which they walked past. Even after careful observation, Marketus couldn't say what made the paths they followed the right ones.

Marketus was so engrossed in the journey and the conversation that he was surprised when Archimedes stopped and said, "Several hours have passed. It's been a long day for you, and the sun will soon set. We'll rest here for the night. You will want plenty of energy for tomorrow."

Then he showed Marketus a nearby stream of crisp, clean water. He demonstrated how to create a comfortable sleeping place from the moss growing beside the path. Then he went to gather fruits and nuts from the surrounding trees for the next day's breakfast.

When Archimedes returned, he opened the satchel full of newly gathered food and took from it a small loaf of bread and a triangle of sharp cheese. He and Marketus ate their dinner of bread, cheese, and ripe blackberries as the sun set.

By the time they'd finished, the forest was dark, lit only by a quarter moon and a sea of stars. Marketus lay down and studied the patterns in the sky.

"What do you find yourself thinking about?" Archimedes asked.

"How many paths there seem to be. Where they go. Where this quest will take me," Marketus answered. He hesitated, then asked, "Are you going to stick around for my whole journey?"

"I will be with you long enough for you to become your own guide," Archimedes said.

"I'm not sure what that means," Marketus said.

Archimedes smiled but offered nothing more. So Marketus took the Tessamark from his pocket and absently ran his finger over the strange object while he thought about what might lie ahead.

Archimedes watched Marketus's deep contemplation for a few minutes, then said, "Congratulations."

"What for?"

"For discovering the first purpose of the Tessamark: reminding you to stop and think—to reflect on your experiences and the lessons they offer."

"That doesn't seem like such a big deal."

"No, it doesn't seem so," replied Archimedes. "Where you come from, people want to do things as quickly as possible—even several things at once. They often believe that simple thought and reflection are a waste of time. But your quest will be much more useful if you occasionally take a break to contemplate your experiences and the world you are traveling through."

Marketus indicated that he understood. A few minutes later, he dropped off to sleep.

LESSON:

Always remember to stop and think—to **REFLECT ON YOUR EXPERIENCES** and the lessons they offer.

CHAPTER TWO

THE VILLAGE OF PASSIONS

Marketus woke the next morning just as the sun broke the horizon. He felt refreshed, with a clear mind, ready to resume his journey. Archimedes laid out the remainder of the nuts and fruits he'd gathered the night before, and the two ate. Then they set off again, walking at a leisurely pace. After an hour, they reached a wooden bridge over a shallow stream. Archimedes pointed to the water and said, "That is the great River Zoe."

Marketus laughed. "Your great river looks more like a nice little creek."

Archimedes smiled. "True. I should have said that this stream *becomes* the great Zoe, the grand and challenging river that courses through the heart of this land." He paused, then continued with quiet intensity. "Our journey will take us through the heart of this land, too. Along the way we will explore four villages. In each, you will be offered something of great value. Observe closely. Listen carefully. Take time to think about what you have seen and heard. Remember: the success of this quest—and of your many future journeys—depends on how well you use what is offered in these villages."

"I will do my best," Marketus replied.

"The entrance to the first village is just down this trail. Before we visit it, I have something for you." Archimedes reached into his satchel and took out a small silk bag tied with gold thread, then handed it to Marketus. "Take care: what is inside is very small and very precious."

Marketus opened the bag and stared at its contents. "A pea?" he asked. "A dried green pea?"

"No normal pea, I assure you," Archimedes said. "Take out the Tessamark and carefully place the pea into the small indentation above the center."

Marketus did as instructed, then gasped in surprise as the indentation closed tightly around the edge of the pea—which then looked like a glowing green pearl.

"I know you have questions, but for now," Archimedes instructed, "place the Tessamark back in your pocket, and let us venture into the first village."

Marketus did as Archimedes advised. "What is the name of this village?" he asked.

"It is called the Village of Passions."

Marketus laughed. "The Village of Passions—where your wildest fantasies come true?"

"Sorry, no," Archimedes replied. "Passions as in: What motivates you? What ideas and activities energize you?"

"That's less enticing," Marketus quipped.

"Nevertheless, how would you answer those questions?" Archimedes asked.

Marketus considered. "There are lots of things I really like to do. I've never thought of them as passions."

"Then we are in exactly the right place. For it is your true passions that will drive you forward in life. They will be the basis for goals you set. And the energy and determination you derive from them will enable you to overcome many obstacles and disappointments," Archimedes said.

Then he and Marketus crossed the bridge and followed the path over a hill and around a bend. Before them stood a tall stone arch that marked the beginning of the Village of Passions. They stopped to admire the arch and the scenery around it.

Just then a woman emerged from an adjacent small building, smiling broadly when she saw the travelers. Archimedes smiled back.

"This is the Village Guide," he told Marketus. "She will offer valuable advice as you begin your explorations."

"It's nice to meet you," Marketus said.

"I'm glad to meet you, too," she responded.

Then Marketus took a closer look at the arch. He noted that it was covered in detailed carvings, each representing an area of human activity or enterprise. There were symbols for almost every undertaking or occupation

Marketus could think of. "Somebody certainly put a lot of time and energy into these carvings," he observed.

"It's how we do things here—with commitment and vigor," said the Village Guide. "Are you a first-time visitor?"

"He is indeed," Archimedes replied. "We wish to explore your village and observe the passions prevalent in its residents' lives."

"Allow me to give you a map to guide you," the woman said. "The village is much larger than you might expect." She ducked into the building, brought out a thick parchment, and unrolled what proved to be several yards of an intricately drawn map. She pointed out the village's primary streets and lanes and some of its scenic spots.

Then she said to Marketus, "I suggest, young man, that on this first visit you skip the neighborhoods marked in blue ink."

"Why?" Marketus asked.

"There are many kinds of passions," the woman explained. "Those that are productive and constructive and those that are not. There are passions one controls and directs, and then there are those that are difficult to control, even addictive. As an ancient sage once said, 'Some passions nurture and feed; some passions know only greed.' The blue-ink neighborhoods are those where people pursue negative passions. Another time, when you have more knowledge and experience, you could visit those areas."

Detail from the
Map of the
Village of Passions

"You are wise and good-hearted," Archimedes said to the woman. "Guiding people is clearly one of your own passions."

In reply, the woman simply smiled, bowed, and directed the visitors toward the village's main street.

The village was organized as a series of neighborhoods, each comprising clusters of houses, communal spaces, and workplaces. And each was populated by people whose lives revolved around a single passion—one that gave them energy and that they were deeply committed to. Archimedes and Marketus spent a few hours in each of these neighborhoods, closely observing the residents and their activities.

In the first neighborhood, people were passionate about science. Some wanted to know how light rays moved; others wanted to know how chemical elements interacted; still others wanted to know how the human body performed its many functions. Each group had erected a building dedicated to its particular field of interest or area of scientific inquiry.

In a nearby neighborhood lived engineers who were passionate about applying scientists' discoveries in practical ways. Marketus was fascinated and might have spent a whole day among them had there not been so much else to explore.

"Engineering may prove to be one of your passions," Archimedes said. "But our purpose now is to explore the broad range of passions, not to dive deeply into any one of them."

Leaving the engineers' realm, they entered the neighborhood where people created visual art. In one building, artists painted every subject imaginable. In another, they sketched intricate drawings with pen and ink. In another, they sculpted huge figures made of stone, and in another, they blew delicate glass figurines.

In a nearby neighborhood, Marketus found buildings where musicians played trumpets and violins, sang songs, wrote symphonies, made recordings, and built musical instruments. After listening to a group of a cappella singers improvising a tune, Marketus said, "I love listening to all kinds of music, but I don't think I've got any real talent for making it."

"I share your predicament," Archimedes replied. "In fact, there are several things I feel passionately about but haven't pursued because I have no particular aptitude for them." He hesitated. "Or maybe I should say that I'm not passionate enough about those things to keep focusing a lot of energy on them."

"Interesting. I never thought about it that way," Marketus said.

"Some people are lucky enough to find a perfect match," Archimedes said. "They are passionate about one thing in particular, do it well, and live in a place where they can earn a living doing it. For those people, many of life's choices are clear.

"But things are more complex for the rest of us," he added. "We have several different passions that grow and diminish over time. Our talents don't necessarily match our passions. And our communities may not reward our specific passions. So the first step for you is to be crystal clear about the things that are most important to you— beginning with recognizing your true passions."

"How do I do that?" Marketus asked.

"I'll explain soon enough," Archimedes said. "But for now, let's call it a day."

Indeed, the sun was low in the sky. Archimedes guided Marketus to a small lodge—a cozy and inviting wooden cottage nestled in a grove of trees—where they had a hot meal and slept in real beds.

―――――――――

Over the course of the next two days, they visited many neighborhoods, observing villagers engaged in a seemingly endless variety of passions—including many that Marketus never knew existed. Just seeing the huge variety was an education in itself.

On the third afternoon, Archimedes pointed to a spot on the map and said, "Marketus, you deserve a little respite. Let's wander over to this neighborhood."

"What's the passion there?"

"Desserts," Archimedes said, patting his stomach with a chuckle.

Half an hour later, sitting in a building where people cooked every conceivable kind of sweet treat, Marketus had wolfed down three fruit pastries before Archimedes had finished his first one. Then Marketus stood and said to his companion, "Take your time and enjoy your pastry. I'm going to explore on my own a little."

Archimedes gave Marketus a searching look, then returned to his pastry.

Two hours later, Marketus returned. Archimedes was not surprised to see a pained look on the young man's face.

"You visited one of the neighborhoods of addictive and unconstructive passions, didn't you?" Archimedes asked in an understanding tone.

Marketus simply nodded and sat down.

"You were not prepared for what you saw."

Marketus shook his head.

"People like to believe that they can fully control every choice they make. But that's not always the case," Archimedes observed. "Sometimes our passions override what logic and experience say is best. That's part of being human."

The two sat silently for a bit. Then Archimedes said, "Put this behind you for now." He unrolled the map to its full length across the floor. "We've only visited a fraction of the village. But a fraction is enough to help you realize how many kinds of passions there are. And to see that one can pursue almost any passion, if one is willing to invest the time and energy."

"I'm beginning to understand," Marketus said. "More than that, I can see that I've ignored some of my own passions—"

"Or simply didn't recognize them," Archimedes interjected.

"Right. Because I didn't know what to call them or how to act on them until I saw people pursuing them."

Marketus thought for a bit, then said, "You know, it just occurred to me: Do these people spend all their lives in one neighborhood?"

"Ah, an excellent question," Archimedes responded. "Some people have a passion that's so fulfilling that they do stay in one neighborhood. However, most of the residents of this village have more than one passion. So they move from neighborhood to neighborhood every few years or just divide their days or weeks among several neighborhoods.

"That's what's wonderful about the Village of Passions," Archimedes continued. "There are no expectations and no restrictions. Residents are free to pursue whatever activity motivates them as long as it doesn't harm another person. And all residents are guaranteed the resources needed to pursue their passions. So here, there are never too many pie makers or bankers or soccer players."

Marketus shook his head. "It's not like that where I'm from."

"True. In your land, there can be many barriers to pursuing your passions. Ultimately, the most important barrier is that there's simply never enough time. So you must prioritize.

"Now, you may feel that setting priorities limits your future opportunities. But not setting priorities often leaves you just meandering from path to path—never feeling satisfied with what you're pursuing, always thinking you should be pursuing something else."

———————

The two visitors spent another day wandering through the village, guided solely by what appealed to Marketus. Several times, they returned to neighborhoods he'd found particularly interesting and wanted to explore further. He would ask the residents which other neighborhoods they frequented and how they balanced—or combined—their several passions.

Finally, the sun fell behind the surrounding hilltops, and Archimedes said, "It is time to continue our journey." They left through a gate on the opposite side of the village from the one through which they'd entered.

From there, they followed a trail that brought them to a broad, gently flowing river that reflected the orange-red sunset. "It's beautiful here," Marketus said. "Is that the River Zoe?"

Archimedes chuckled. "Yes. Remember the little creek we crossed a few days ago? This is what it looks like after it's been fed by a series of underground springs."

Archimedes took from his satchel a ball of thin twine, a leather pouch containing three fishhooks, and a small piece of bread he had saved from their morning meal to use as bait. "Fishing is a passion I can only rarely indulge. But tonight, passion and necessity come together: I will catch our meal while you build a fire."

As Marketus gathered firewood, Archimedes prepared his fishing lines, and soon the two sat beside a small fire while their meal cooked. "All in all," Marketus said, "I would love to live in a place where I could pursue all my passions as often or as seldom as I want—as soon as I figure out what they are."

Archimedes said, "Well, the first step in that process is straightforward. Ask yourself four simple questions: First, what activities make time pass quickly? Second, what subjects do I hunger to learn about? Third, what tasks do I pursue with commitment and energy, without hesitation? And fourth, what do I daydream about?"

Marketus repeated each of the questions. Then he said, "Yup. That's pretty simple."

"Important questions aren't necessarily complicated," Archimedes responded. "It is in answering them that complications begin."

"But don't other things matter, too, besides my passions? Like what I'm good at? What I believe in? My personality?"

"Those matter a great deal," Archimedes replied, "especially as you make choices about which passions to pursue, how much energy to devote to each, and what trade-offs you'll accept in order to pursue them. But the starting point is *identifying* your passions."

"You're saying that passions are more important than strengths and weaknesses, skills and talents?" Marketus asked.

"They're more fundamental. Passions, skills, and strengths are often inextricably linked, like the chicken and the egg. It's hard to know which comes first. But where they diverge, you must start with passions, which will always be your most powerful driver. And you must always be aware of what you're giving up in not pursuing a passion."

Marketus considered his point, then asked, "What if my answers to those four simple questions change over time?"

"Inevitably, they will. As your life progresses, some passions will remain; others will evolve or even dissolve completely and be replaced by new ones," Archimedes answered. "Some passions you are born with. They're in your genes and will stay with you. Others you will discover in your future journeys—much like the fruits we've encountered in our walks through the forest. And throughout your life, the way you view your passions will be affected by your environment—by the culture and society and economy that shape your day-to-day world. We'll talk more about all those things as this quest goes on. But regardless of the changes that take place within or around you, simply answer the four questions as honestly as you can, based on what you know at the time, and act on those answers."

Their conversation paused while they ate the fish and a loaf of bread they had bought in the village. After dinner, Marketus rummaged through his backpack and pulled out the Tessamark. "I've been wondering about this," he said. "When will we turn it on?"

"It's been working since you placed the first pea in it," Archimedes replied. "The Tessamark is a nexus. It gathers the intellectual energy created when you consider important questions or when something powerful motivates you. Then it can read that intellectual energy back to you in a clear and organized manner."

"How can it 'read' back to me?" Marketus asked.

"See for yourself," Archimedes responded. "Place your finger on the Passions Pea and think about what you have learned and experienced in the Village of Passions."

Marketus did as he was told. After a moment, the Tessamark vibrated slightly, then projected a vertical screen of light directly before him. On the screen were the thoughts he'd just had in his mind:

I have a passion for music—*but no real talent.*

I may have a passion for engineering—*but I need to explore it more.*

I like exploring new places—*but is that a passion?*

I really like collaborating on projects with other people—*but how does that fit with my other passions?*

"Wow! It reads my mind!" Marketus said.

"It gathers thoughts in which you have invested intellectual or emotional energy," Archimedes explained. "Initially, it will help you view, consider, and compare all the passions you've identified. In the next stages of your quest, you'll place three more peas in the Tessamark. Then you will really see what it can do."

"Pretty cool," Marketus said as he turned the Tessamark over in his hand. "Where does its power come from? Some tiny battery?"

Archimedes laughed. "No battery. The Tessamark is driven solely by your intellectual and emotional energies. And as you pursue this quest, you'll see it grow in power."

With that, Archimedes turned to check the fire. Then he lay down, using his satchel as a pillow. "I suggest that we get some sleep. Tomorrow will require a strenuous hike—not the leisurely walks we've enjoyed so far."

KEY IDEAS AND QUESTIONS

PASSIONS are the powerful interests that drive us forward in life. They should be the starting point for the plans we create.

Our **PASSIONS AND OUR STRENGTHS** are often closely linked, and that can be powerful. But where they diverge, we should concentrate on our passions.

THERE CAN BE PRACTICAL BARRIERS to pursuing our passions—including time, cost, and knowledge.

PASSIONS DO NOT NECESSARILY LAST FOREVER: some will last, others will morph, and new passions may arise.

1. **What are your passions?**

2. **Which of them is most important to you?**

3. **What are your areas
   of strength, skill, and talent?**

4. **Which of them overlap with your
   passions and which do not?**

5. **What barriers might interfere with
   your pursuing each of your passions?**

6. **How might you overcome those barriers?**

7. **Have you experienced
   changes in your passions?**

8. **Have these changes affected
   the way you think about your future?**

CHAPTER THREE

THE VILLAGE OF PRINCIPLES

The next morning, Marketus woke up early, raring to go. After a hearty breakfast of toast and porridge, he strolled out into the sunshine and admired the tall peaks in the vista above him. It was a beautiful day, and he felt as if he was about to learn something new.

Archimedes pointed to the highest peak and told Marketus that was their challenge of the day. Marketus wasn't sure it was possible to climb it. But he was game to try, assured by Archimedes that it was easier than it looked.

But the hike up the mountain was a lot tougher than he thought it would be. In many places, the trail angled sharply upward, forcing Marketus and Archimedes to strain and struggle as they climbed higher and higher. It took impressive agility to manage this climb. In some cases, they had to maneuver from boulder to boulder or cross over unstable rocks. It seemed to Marketus that every step required a new decision.

For the most part, he was able to follow Archimedes's path. But at several points—because he was less experienced than his guide—he had to take an easier, more time-consuming detour from the most direct path. Archimedes patiently waited for Marketus to figure out the route that worked best for him, then they continued on together.

Reaching a village just as the sun set, they headed directly to a large mountain lodge built of red brick, where there was a fire going in each of the main rooms on the first floor. It was the most welcoming place imaginable, with comfortable chairs and couches and wonderful aromas coming out of the open kitchen. The travelers ate a hot meal of roast beef and potatoes, followed by apple pie, then went right to sleep.

The next morning, Marketus found that the village stood on a broad plateau on the mountainside. Looking back toward the valley out of which they'd hiked, he could see the walls surrounding the Village of Passions, the meandering River Zoe, and—in the distance—the ocean that had brought him to this fascinating land. Turning back around, Marketus saw that the plateau was studded with homes, shops, lodges, and other small buildings. Beyond them lay orchards, fields, and farms. And past them, the mountain rose again.

"We didn't talk much on our hike yesterday," he said to Archimedes. "I don't even know what this place is called."

"I didn't want to break your concentration during our challenging climb," Archimedes replied. "This is the Village of Principles. We will spend several days here. There is much to explore."

"Really?" Marketus said. "It seems small compared to the Village of Passions."

"What you now see—the buildings, the fields—are but a portion of the village," Archimedes said. "Its exploration will be more challenging than the Village of Passions."

"Will it be as tough as yesterday?" Marketus asked.

"Yesterday was physically difficult. Your tasks here will be challenging intellectually and spiritually," Archimedes responded. "Some of these explorations will come naturally to you. Others will require you to wrestle with complex ideas and deep-rooted assumptions." He stopped to watch a bird glide high over the plateau. "In the Village of Principles you will consider four questions: *What do I believe? How will I conduct myself based on those beliefs? What rules will I follow? What lines will I not cross?*"

As Marketus came to understand, the Village of Principles had many layers. That first morning, he and Archimedes simply wandered across the plateau—browsing in the general store, watching the village's Blacksmith at work, walking through a few orchards.

Archimedes took the afternoon off for rest and contemplation. Marketus decided to trek along the plateau's outer edge, and as he was taking in the view of the surrounding valleys, a solidly built man came sauntering down the path. It was the Blacksmith, whom Marketus and Archimedes had observed that morning.

The Blacksmith stopped and looked at Marketus quizzically, then said, "Ah, that's right. You're Archimedes's young companion. Where have you come from?" Marketus began to tell the story of his voyage across the ocean, but the man stopped him with a gentle hand on the shoulder. "Yes, my boy, I know. But is this the first stop on your quest? Or did you begin elsewhere?"

"We've come from the Village of Passions," Marketus replied.

"Good, good. There are many who believe our village should be the first stop on anyone's visit. They have good reasons to think so and could be right," the burly man said. "But I believe that, realistically speaking, passions come first. Principles and values complement and add shape to your passions. Of course, you might expect nothing else from a Blacksmith: shaping and honing are what I do," he observed with a laugh. "If you have time, come see me after you've explored the higher realms of our village. Tell me what you make of them."

"Yes, I will," Marketus said. The Blacksmith nodded and walked on.

That evening, Marketus mentioned the Blacksmith's suggestion to Archimedes, who replied, "Excellent. We shall be sure to visit him. But tomorrow, you begin exploring the most important part of the village."

———————

Marketus and Archimedes were up with the sun, and after breakfast, they walked to the plateau's northern side, where the mountain rose again. There they found a long stairway carved into the mountainside and began to climb. Eventually, the stairway curved into the mountain itself, through a wide passage hewn in the rock. There Marketus saw a broad stone floor beneath an ornately decorated ceiling that arced across an enormous space. The huge room was brightly lit, with many small windows admitting sunlight through the outer walls.

"What is this place?" Marketus asked, amazed.

"This is the antechamber to the Temple of Philosophy and Morality," Archimedes replied. "It is the heart and soul of the village." He pointed across the cavern to a long semicircular inner wall that held a series of arches. "The temple comprises several individual halls reached through those arched passageways. Each hall includes many separate rooms and alcoves."

Marketus saw that a name was carved above each arch and read a few out loud. "Hall of Religion;

Hall of Cosmology; Hall of Psychology; Hall of . . . Superterrestriality? Nanophilology? What are those?"

"The temple is a living library that captures the many ways humans think about their place in the world," Archimedes said. "In each hall are gathered together philosophical and moral approaches that share a common theme.

"The Hall of Religion, for example, is a series of rooms, each dedicated to a single religious tradition. And many of those rooms have several alcoves within them, each focusing on a different branch of that religion."

"How many halls are there?"

"Currently, several dozen—but the number changes as humanity's understanding of the world evolves."

"And how many rooms and alcoves in all?"

"Innumerable," Archimedes responded. "I have not yet come to the end of them, and I've visited many times."

Marketus looked around the large antechamber. "So what do I do here?"

"Explore," Archimedes answered. "Test. Consider."

"Test and consider what?"

"Test how you see the world—in comparison to the way others view it. Test your beliefs and assumptions. Test what happens when you use unfamiliar lenses to view the world. Consider the values and principles that guide the way you interact with the world. Consider how you put those principles into action from day to day."

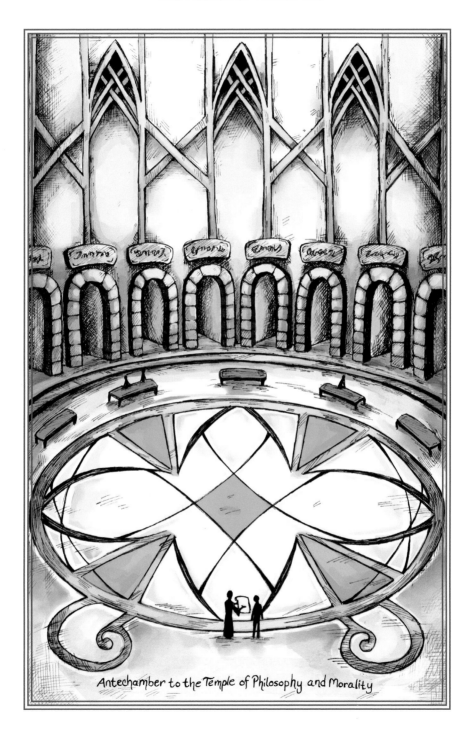

Antechamber to the Temple of Philosophy and Morality

Archimedes let Marketus absorb that, then went on. "Ultimately, your goal here is to begin identifying the principles most important to you."

Marketus gazed across at the arched entryways. "But if this temple is as big as you say, we could be here for weeks," he said.

"You don't need to experience everything now. Just explore enough to allow you to recognize the great number of philosophies and moral systems that exist. Get a sense of the great variety of values and principles you could choose among. You need not make any final decisions now. Indeed, many people never really finish exploring their beliefs. I, for example, continually reexamine my principles and values in light of new experiences and new perspectives. However, what you absorb in the next several days will form the foundation of your own beliefs and ethical system."

Marketus took a deep breath and said, "Okay, where do I start?"

"Start just by asking yourself what you believe and why. Don't try to create an exhaustive list. Simply reflect on your most important principles and why you hold them. Then wander into the halls." He reached into his satchel, removed a roll of parchment, and handed it to Marketus. "This map of the temple will help you. But I suggest that you let curiosity guide you whenever possible."

Marketus studied the map for a moment. When he looked up again, Archimedes held out a small silk bag tied with silver thread and said, "You'll want to use this, too."

Marketus carefully opened the bag and removed the dry, lusterless pea it contained. He took the Tessamark from his pocket and placed the pea in the indentation on the right; with a pearly green glow, it melded with the device.

Without hesitating, Marketus put his thumb on the Principles Pea, and after a moment a screen of light emerged from the Tessamark. The screen held an odd assortment of phrases, words, and symbols—nothing like the clear thoughts it displayed after he and Archimedes had left the Village of Passions. "It's pretty much gibberish," Marketus noted.

"Although you have some principles, they are not deeply thought through," Archimedes pointed out. "You have adopted them but not considered them closely. Before the Tessamark can read back coherent thoughts, you need to invest mental energy. Your explorations in the Temple will help." Then Archimedes took a small canvas sack from his satchel. "Something to eat and drink," he offered. "You'll be here most of the day, I expect."

"What about you?" Marketus asked.

"I am going to visit the Blacksmith," Archimedes replied.

"But all these halls and rooms—even with this map I'm bound to get lost."

"Don't worry. There are guides in each room; they'll answer your questions and help you interpret the map. Also, your Tessamark will track your progress. Use it with the map to retrace your steps back here."

———————

Marketus spent a long day exploring the Temple of Philosophy and Morality. He started in the Hall of Religion because those ideas were most familiar to him. Its individual rooms spanned the entire alphabet—from Akom, Buddhism, and Christianity to Hinduism, Islam, and Judaism to Sikhism, Taoism, and Zoroastrianism.

Throughout his wanderings, he took in ideas, asked questions, and tried to keep everything straight in his mind—a challenging task, given how much information he was taking in.

At day's end, Marketus descended the mountainside stairway from the temple's antechamber to the plateau. Though physically exhausted, his mind was full of energy. Over dinner at another lodge, which also had excellent food, he told Archimedes about the many ideas and people he'd encountered.

"There were people in every hall and room, and I spoke with some of them about their beliefs and principles. A few seemed very knowledgeable; most others were asking questions, just as I was," Marketus recalled. Then he wondered, "Where did they all come from? I haven't seen that many people around the village."

"A few of those you saw today are village residents. They are the scholars, guides, and caretakers of the temple," Archimedes explained. "All the rest were visitors, like you, contemplating the fundamental principles that guide the way they live their lives. Most stay in special lodges secluded on the mountainside; each lodge is dedicated to one hall and connected to it by a direct path through the mountain."

"Does that make it difficult for them to explore other halls if they want to?"

"Not really," Archimedes replied. "Look carefully tomorrow, and you'll find many intersections—places where a room in a hall connects directly to a similarly focused room in another hall. It's fascinating and valuable to see how many systems of belief connect with one another, in ways large and small."

Marketus spent three more full days wandering from hall to hall and room to room—deeply investigating some, passing quickly through others. But midway through his fifth day of exploration, his mental energy ran out. He couldn't contemplate one more idea, value, principle, or connection. So he made his way back down to the plateau and found a comfortable spot outdoors under a tree; there he sat and let his mind wander. His thoughts circled from the valleys to the hills to the clouds to the interesting ideas he'd encountered. He knew that the Tessamark would capture whatever questions or conclusions his mind formed for future consideration.

After dinner that night at the lodge, Marketus turned to Archimedes and said, "We've talked a lot about my beliefs and principles, but not much about yours. Why not?"

Archimedes smiled. "I didn't want my perspectives to sway your explorations. But I will gladly share my principles with you now."

Marketus settled back in his chair. "Okay. It must be a long list, given how often you've been here."

"Actually, I have just a few fundamental principles that guide my plans and decisions," Archimedes said. "I've found that having a large number of specific principles is not useful; it's hard to keep track of them and hard to adapt them when things change. They too easily become barriers or constraints rather than what they should be."

"Which is . . ."

"Guidelines for living your life and pursuing your passions. As our friend the Blacksmith would say, principles should shape and focus a person's passions. So I have only three of them." Archimedes then listed them in order.

PRINCIPLE NUMBER ONE:
Treat others as you hope to be treated.

PRINCIPLE NUMBER TWO:
Seek freedom to make your own decisions.

PRINCIPLE NUMBER THREE:
Decide what's enough—enough money, possessions, accomplishments, recognition, engagement, and love—and don't pursue more than enough.

Marketus considered those principles, then asked, "But what about doctrines such as 'Don't kill' and 'Don't steal'?"

Archimedes replied, "They are important values that, for me, fit within 'Treat others as you hope to be treated.'"

With that, Archimedes walked with Marketus to his room at the lodge, and then bid his young companion goodnight, and left him to his thoughts.

The next morning, Archimedes announced, "Today will be dedicated to physical labor. It will balance out all the deep thinking you've been doing."

He and Marketus spent the day working in the village's orchards, filling dozens of baskets with apples, pears, and peaches. They were each compensated with a small sack of fruit. "We will enjoy these when we resume our journey tomorrow," Archimedes said.

"You think I've absorbed enough from the temple?" Marketus asked as they walked out of the orchard.

"You will be absorbing for many days to come—digesting the array of ideas and precepts you have encountered," Archimedes said.

"Letting my principles ripen like fruit," Marketus mused.

"Exactly," Archimedes replied. "For now, though, the Blacksmith has invited us to dinner. So let's see what interesting desserts the bakery has to offer."

That evening, after a nourishing dinner at the Blacksmith's, the three men enjoyed a dessert of peach pie, which was baked that afternoon with fruit picked that morning. "Wonderful," said the Blacksmith, leaning back in his chair. "You know, the Baker has a very particular way with ingredients. He doesn't always use them exactly the same way. His recipes vary slightly from season to season."

"Why is that?" Marketus asked.

"It is a bedrock principle of his to make the best-tasting pie possible at all times. For him, putting that principle into action means using slightly different recipes as the changing seasons alter the way the peaches taste. Or maybe it's that the seasons change the way our taste buds work. Or maybe—ahh, no matter," the Blacksmith said, waving his hand. "The point is the same." He pulled his chair closer to Marketus's. "It's all well and good to think about the principles guiding your life. The next challenge—often the bigger challenge—is deciding how to put your principles into action, day after day.

"So let me ask you," the Blacksmith continued. "How do your principles directly affect the way you interact with the people around you? How do you translate your principles into conduct?"

Marketus thought for a while, then said, "I guess I have some rules that guide my actions. I don't intentionally hurt people, for example. But I haven't connected those rules directly with my fundamental principles."

The Blacksmith nodded. "Then it's something to consider as your quest continues. And I think you'll find it has a nice circular effect: figuring out how to put a principle into action helps you decide if you really want to adopt it. Do you follow me?" the Blacksmith asked. "What's the point of my adopting a particular principle if I'm not willing to act on it? That would just leave me feeling frustrated or hypocritical."

Marketus looked at Archimedes. "So is there a Temple of Rules and Actions I can go to to help me think those things through?"

Archimedes smiled and shook his head. "No. But you can create something like it by paying attention to the way other people put their principles to work, comparing their approaches to your own, and building on what you observe."

The Blacksmith added, "The rules and actions you create must be your own because they are based on the mix of principles and circumstances unique to you. But I can tell you how I've approached it."

"Yes, please do," Marketus said.

"I'm what you'd call a physical thinker. I like to see things in front of me," the Blacksmith began. "So I lay my most important beliefs and principles on the table using tools or other objects to represent my ideas. You know—my hammer represents the principle of hard work. A coin represents the principle of giving people fair value for their money, and so on. Then I ask myself: How does each of these principles apply to the key realms of my life?"

"Key realms?" Marketus asked.

The Blacksmith said, "Let me draw it for you." He grabbed the piece of heavy paper the pie had been wrapped in, pulled a well-used pencil from his vest pocket, and proceeded to draw a chart. Along the left side he listed his principles; across the top he wrote brief descriptions of the four realms:

> **SELF**—the capacity to be introspective and to understand myself and therefore maintain a sense of self-worth, self-confidence, and day-to-day happiness
>
> **FAMILY**—the way I love, nurture, and enjoy the people closest to me
>
> **WORK**—the way I financially support myself and my family and realize a sense of professional achievement
>
> **COMMUNITY**—the willingness to use my time and energy to give back to others

"I line up the four realms next to each principle and think about what it means to act out the principle in each realm," the Blacksmith said.

"Thanks," Marketus replied. "That could be a useful way to think about the most important parts of my life." He paused. "Should all principles apply to all those realms—and in the same way?"

"In my experience, it's not necessary to connect everything," the Blacksmith replied. "And no, often they don't apply the same way. Consider a principle I know Archimedes and I share—'Seek freedom'—and one of my own, which is 'Work hard each day.' The way I seek freedom in the work realm, for example, is that I run my own business and only accept as many projects as I know I can complete between breakfast and dinner. That leaves my nights free. That's also how I ensure that I work hard each day—by not accepting fewer jobs than will fill my day."

"And how do you address your seek-freedom principle in the community realm?" Marketus wondered.

"Good question!" the Blacksmith replied. "One way I engage with my community is by being a guide in the temple two days a month. But I choose which two days and in which of the halls I'll be stationed." Then he leaned forward and said in a confidential tone, "I'll also tell you this: 'Seek freedom' may be my most important principle. So some days I will skip work altogether, hike down the valley, and spend a few hours fishing."

"I'm sure there are days that Archimedes would love to do just that," Marketus joked.

"Indeed there are," Archimedes said with a laugh. "And our friend makes a point you should remember: there are times when acting on one principle may mean not acting on another. You'll need to consider how to prioritize them."

"And," the Blacksmith said, "that process of evaluating and balancing and prioritizing your principles and actions—that process never really ends, my boy." He watched as Marketus absorbed his point. "That sounds daunting, I know, but it's one of the things that makes life interesting. I mean, where's the fun in playing a game that's simple and easy to win all the time?"

Marketus then sat back and became lost in thought. After a few moments, the older men moved into the house. From time to time, Marketus could hear them laughing about some shared experience. But mostly, his mind was far away, considering the principles that guided his life and how they related to one another and to his actions.

Later that night, Marketus took the Tessamark from his pocket and put a finger on the Principles Pea. The light screen showed him a set of principles that, while not fully formed, were coherent and clear. It even captured some rules for acting on those principles. He considered the screen for a few minutes. Then he had an idea.

———

Recounting the experience to Archimedes the next morning, Marketus said, "Last night I wondered what would happen if I activated the Passion Pea and the Principles Pea at the same time. So I did, and it was amazing! First the Tessamark produced a screen that listed my passions—which included a few ideas that were different from those I'd seen when I last looked at them. Then the Principles screen came up beside it, and they started blending together. It was little confusing, but I think it was cross-referencing the two sets of information."

"You are observant—that is exactly what it was doing," Archimedes said. "Integrating your principles and passions is essential to defining who you are and how you will interact with the world. It's especially important in helping you make choices that involve weighing and balancing many factors in your life."

"What kind of choices?" Marketus asked.

"Let's say that you conclude today that passion A is your strongest passion and that principle 1 is your most important principle. So what happens if tomorrow you discover that putting principle 1 into action makes pursuing passion A more difficult? Or that they're in outright conflict? Perhaps you choose to pursue another passion, at least for the time being. Or maybe you change how you put principle 1 into action."

Then Archimedes took a more serious tone. "This is very important, because life will require you to make many such choices. The more thoughtful and conscious you can be in making those choices, the more effective and satisfying they'll be. Do you understand what I'm saying?"

"Yes," Marketus said.

"Next time you use the Tessamark, consciously focus on one item at a time and observe how the relationship among all the elements changes. If you place your finger on the raised circle in the center of the device, it will freeze the image, and you can take your time to assess what you see; remove your finger, and the Tessamark will resume actively reordering the elements according to your focus. In this way, it enables you to consider what is most important for you at any one time and how choices will affect other elements of your life."

Marketus considered this and said, "And that information will help me identify the paths I should take in my life—right?"

Archimedes shook his head. "Not wholly: there is more information you must gather to effectively map out your life's path. The quest continues."

LESSON:

Consciously focus on one item at a time and observe how the relationship among all the elements changes. This will enable you to consider what is most important for you at any one time and how **CHOICES WILL AFFECT OTHER ELEMENTS OF YOUR LIFE.**

KEY IDEAS AND QUESTIONS

YOUR PRINCIPLES help define
the kind of person you are and
the way you live your life.

PRINCIPLES COMPLEMENT YOUR PASSIONS,
shaping the way you pursue them.

For our principles to be meaningful,
we must act on them in the
FOUR KEY REALMS OF OUR LIVES:
Self, Family, Work, and Community.

We must **CONTINUALLY REEXAMINE**
our principles in light of new experiences
and new perspectives.

And we should **TEST WAYS OF VIEWING**
the world other than those
we typically use.

1. **What are the fundamental principles guiding your life?**

2. **Which of them is most important to you?**

3. **How do your principles affect how you pursue your passions?**

4. **Are there any conflicts between your principles and passions?**

5. **How do you apply your principles in each realm?**

6. **How might you apply them in the future?**

7. **Have you had experiences that changed the way you view the world and prompted you to reconsider any of your principles?**

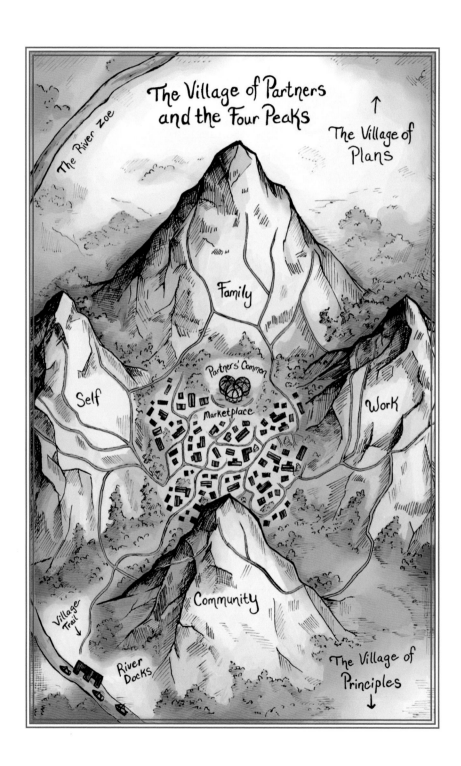

CHAPTER FOUR

THE VILLAGE OF PARTNERS

Marketus and Archimedes came down the mountain by a different route from the one they'd climbed to reach the Village of Principles. Soon the steep rocky path gave way to grassy fields, then to long, leaf-cushioned trails through thick forest. When they finally emerged from the trees, they stood at the edge of a huge gorge. Hundreds of feet below, a broad, fast-flowing river snaked through a long, curving valley.

"Do you recognize it?" Archimedes asked. "The River Zoe—once a trickle, now a great torrent that will carry us to the next village. I've arranged for a boat to take us."

Marketus peered over the cliff edge uncertainly. "How do we get down there?"

"Follow me," Archimedes replied.

They walked a short distance along a cliffside path until they reached a sturdy wooden platform cantilevered over the cliff. In the platform's center was a sling

chair connected to a system of ropes, pulleys, and levers. The chair was poised over a square opening; through it another platform could be seen thirty feet down. Two more platforms sat below that one.

"This series of platforms will enable us to descend to the river," Archimedes said. "The chair mechanism is designed for two people working together, each lowering the other in turn." He explained in detail how the process worked. Marketus listened carefully, rehearsed the steps in his mind, and repeated back the instructions.

"You've got it. But before we begin, please take out your Tessamark," Archimedes said. Then he removed from his satchel a small silk bag tied with a crimson ribbon and held it out to Marketus. "This is the Partners Pea. Place it in the Tessamark now; our descent to the river is the first of many experiences worth capturing." Marketus carefully took the new pea from the bag, placed it in one of the two remaining indentations on the Tessamark, and watched as it melded into the device with a pearly green glow. "Your experiences in the Villages of Passions and Principles were focused mostly on you. But these next experiences will focus on the people around you. Now tuck the Tessamark away, and let us begin."

Archimedes climbed into the sling chair, and Marketus lowered him to the next platform. The chair was raised back to the top, then Marketus descended. This process was repeated until they reached a wide rock shelf along the riverside.

There, a boat was moored—a cross between cargo barge and white-water raft, designed to carry supplies and passengers down the Zoe. Its crew members were securing newly loaded crates, while off to the side stood two would-be passengers. One, a middle-aged woman, wore a long robe similar to Archimedes's. The other was a young woman around Marketus's age. Seeing Archimedes, the older woman walked to him and said, "Well met, my dear friend. May I speak to you for a moment?" To Marketus, she said, "My name is Xenia. Please forgive my interrupting your journey. But I must ask a great favor."

"No problem. I'll just wait by the boat," Marketus replied.

"Oh, no," the woman said. "This is a favor I ask from you both."

Like Archimedes, Xenia was a guide through the four villages. The young woman she accompanied was named Thalia; Marketus recalled seeing her in the Temple of Philosophy and Morality, but they hadn't met.

Xenia drew all three of them aside and revealed that the previous night she'd received a message from her Prime Partner. She told Thalia and Marketus, "When we first committed ourselves to each other, my P1—that's what I call my Prime Partner—and I agreed that I would continue to serve as a guide, even though it would mean leaving home for weeks at a time. But if there was ever an important reason for me to come home, I would return immediately. I received such a message last night."

She sighed. "In all our years together, this is the first time I have not completed a journey. It is a significant sacrifice for me to relinquish my responsibilities as a guide, even for just a while. It makes me unhappy. But *compromise* and *sacrifice* are building blocks of a Prime Partnership, along with love, respect, and commitment. So if you will permit me, I will ask you, Archimedes, and you, Marketus, to consider accepting a fellow voyager in your travels. I've told Thalia that if, after meeting you, she has any reservations, we will return to the Village of Principles, and I will find a guide she is completely comfortable with."

"For my part, it would be an honor," Archimedes said without hesitation, knowing that anyone Xenia agreed to guide would be smart and dedicated to the quest. "But let us take some time for Marketus and Thalia to consider what it might mean for them."

The four found a place to sit and talk. During the next hour, Thalia and Marketus discussed their backgrounds, recounted their experiences in the Villages of Passions and Principles, and described how those experiences affected their thinking. The four talked about potential challenges that could arise in the journey and how they could be handled. In the end, they all agreed that Thalia would travel with Marketus and Archimedes. Before departing, Xenia transferred a few items from her satchel to Archimedes's. Then she said a heartfelt farewell to Thalia and hurried off on a riverside trail to reconnect with her P1.

A few minutes later, the trio of voyagers took their seats on the boat, and it got underway. When it had maneuvered safely away from the cliffside and into the river flow, a tall man with graying hair and sun-toughened skin sat down with his three passengers. He was Kybernetes, the boat's captain and an old friend of Archimedes. A talkative fellow, Kybernetes kept up a steady banter—alternately pointing out notable landmarks to Marketus and Thalia, updating Archimedes on shared friends' adventures, and discussing the economics of ferrying cargo along the Zoe. Now and then he would draw a crew member's attention to something ahead—an uprooted tree floating along with the current, a small ferryboat crossing their path, or an unexpected patch of turbulent water.

Kybernetes never issued commands. He communicated with his crew using a few quiet words, a hand gesture, or just a nod of the head and a glance in a particular direction.

"You are lucky to have such a good crew: knowing their jobs so well, they give you plenty of time for sightseeing and chitchat," Archimedes said to Kybernetes with a wink.

The captain chuckled and replied, "Yes, lucky. But you know the old saying, 'Luck favors the prepared.' I knew what I was looking for when luck introduced me to each of these folks." One by one, when their duties permitted, Kybernetes brought the women and men of the crew forward to meet their passengers. He described in clear and simple terms each person's job and the skills he or she needed to perform well. He made a point of noting where a crew member's specific ability or knowledge complemented or exceeded his own.

When the introductions concluded, Kybernetes observed, "After all our years together and with all our shared experiences, these people are more my partners than my crew. And there's no substitute for experienced partners when you're navigating this unpredictable and challenging river."

"Why do you say unpredictable and challenging?" Marketus asked. "The river is smooth, and the trip has been very pleasant."

The captain laughed and looked at Archimedes, who shrugged his shoulders and said, "He and Thalia have much to see and experience, Kybernetes. That is why they're on this journey."

"You pay us a compliment in calling this ride pleasant," Kybernetes told Marketus. "It is smooth because this crew is so good at handling strong crosscurrents that could drive us into the cliff. They also know how to avoid submerged boulders that could claw the bottom of the boat and slip around sudden whirlpools that could spin us in dizzying circles. And then, of course," he continued with a mischievous smile, "you've not yet experienced the rapids ahead. They can be quite beautiful to see but quite scary to be tossed about in."

Kybernetes was right. Approaching the rapids, Thalia and Marketus were fascinated by the sight of the rushing, tumbling water. But when the boat entered the white water, it bucked wildly, veering back and forth as the crew navigated the narrow, twisting channels. The young voyagers thought the boat might capsize. But ultimately, they were awed by the crew's ability to handle every challenge thrown at them, especially one or two they hadn't anticipated.

Once they were past the rapids, the river calmed and ran in a nearly straight line toward the ring of mountains known as the Four Peaks. The peaks were four individual mountains that rose in a massive circle. From afar, Thalia suggested, they looked like four giant friends sitting around a table.

The Village of Partners lay in a round valley—a kind of geologic bowl set in the center of the mountains. It was reached by a well-worn trail running from the riverside through a low pass between two of the peaks. After docking, Marketus, Thalia, and Archimedes parted with Kybernetes and his crew, then walked up to the village. It was a busy place, the streets filled with people walking in pairs or small groups, conversing as they went.

The day's journey had been long, so the trio found rooms in a lodge. They ate a filling dinner, then headed for some much-needed sleep.

The next morning, they were pleasantly surprised to find that two of Kybernetes's crew, Cleo and Pegalus, had also slept at the lodge and were preparing to head back to the riverside.

"Where are Kybernetes and the rest of the crew?" Thalia asked.

"Last night, after we unloaded some cargo, they continued downriver. It's relatively easy to navigate, and they won't need our services," Cleo said.

"So what will you do now?" Thalia wondered.

"We'll simply head back upriver," Cleo replied.

"She is being modest; the trip back will not be simple," Pegalus interjected. "But Cleo here is an expert at upriver navigation, and she will captain the boat that returns this morning to the Village of Principles and then to the Village of Passions."

Archimedes elaborated. "It takes a distinct set of skills and knowledge to guide a boat upriver. So while Kybernetes's abilities and experiences perfectly prepare him to captain a downriver trip, he will join someone else's crew for upriver journeys."

"And what about you, Pegalus?" asked Marketus. "What kind of boats do you captain?"

"Oh, I'm good at several crew roles, but I'd be a lousy captain," Pegalus answered. Then, tilting his head at Cleo, he said with a smile, "I'm not half as talented as my P1 here. So I just follow her wherever she goes."

"Actually, he is captain of the 'home ship,'" Cleo said. "He built our house from the ground up, and he cooks virtually all our meals."

"Sounds like you make a great team," Thalia remarked.

"Yes, we do!" said Cleo. "And right now, it's time to put on my captain's hat and prod my crew into action." With that, she and Pegalus said goodbye to the voyagers and set off on the trail to the river.

"Time to start our day's work as well," Archimedes said, reaching into his satchel. He removed two scrolls and gave one each to Marketus and Thalia, who spread them out on the grass. They were maps detailing the village's layout and the main climbing routes up each of the four mountains.

"This says that the Four Peaks are named Self, Family, Work, and Community—the same as the Blacksmith's four realms," Marketus noted.

"Exactly," Archimedes said. "The Blacksmith has traveled more widely than you might have guessed. And he's observed that virtually wherever you live, meeting the challenges of Self, Family, Work, and Community is the main effort of a lifetime. These challenges are reflected in the effort required to climb the Four Peaks: reaching the top of any of these mountains requires determination, endurance, a clear sense of what's important to you, and a healthy dose of good luck—as do the challenges you will encounter in the four realms throughout your lives."

"But what's the connection between the Four Peaks and this village?" Thalia asked. "I mean, this is a beautiful place, and it would be fun to hike in the mountains, but why are we here?"

"Perfect question!" said Archimedes. "Your ability to scale these peaks—how high you climb and how easy that climb is—depends on whether you have the right partners accompanying you. Our visit to the Village of Partners will help you consider the people you'll need to help you ascend the peaks in your lives."

"So the bottom line is that we should have other people along with us when we undertake these challenging climbs," Thalia offered.

"Yes, but not just any group of people," Archimedes responded. "You need a specifically chosen team of partners—people with a particular mix of skills, knowledge, and experiences."

"What mix are we talking about?" Marketus asked.

"That is what you can determine in this part of your quest," Archimedes replied. "Start by asking yourself two questions: What specific capabilities—types of knowledge, skills, tangible resources, and emotional strengths—will I need to go up each of those peaks? And which of those capabilities might I need partners to provide, because I don't have enough—or the right kind—of them myself?"

Archimedes continued, "The best way to answer those questions is to simply jump in: start climbing the foothills, see how you do, observe how other people do, and talk to them about their experiences. Then climb higher and repeat the process."

Archimedes saw that Thalia and Marketus were both unconvinced about the importance of partners. "I understand your skepticism," he said, "because many people from your lands are taught that self-reliance is the most important factor in success—that you should be able to independently handle anything that needs doing.

"But with each passing year, you will better recognize how few things you're really good at and how many things you're not good at. You'll find that even the smartest, most talented people need partners to help when their own experience comes up short.

"We're visiting the Village of Partners to give you a head start in figuring out the kind of partners you'll need in your lives. As you experience the challenge of climbing these peaks, you'll see how valuable it is to find partners who can do certain things that you just can't do. Or who simply do those things better than you do. Or who will happily do things you don't want to do.

"So as you experience these peaks, I'd like you to envision yourselves as lead climbers—individuals who set a goal and surround themselves with a unique team of climbing partners. At the same time, remember that during your lives you'll have opportunities to help other lead climbers by being partners for them—much as Kybernetes and Cleo each captain certain boats but join the crew on other boats."

Archimedes let Marketus and Thalia absorb this. Then he said, "Now, understand, the choosing of partners is not a once-in-a-lifetime decision. But you should identify the kinds of partners you need as early as you can. Then, as you encounter new challenges and possibilities during your climbs, you can seek additional or different partners. I, for example, have often added partners to help with unexpected opportunities and problems."

Thalia frowned and said, "I don't mean to be rude, but I have parents and older sisters and brothers. Aren't they partners? When I get home, aren't they the team that will help me succeed on whatever mountain I choose to climb?"

"Family is very important, Thalia," Archimedes responded. "But there is a place I would like you to see—it will help answer your questions." And so they rolled up their maps and set off to the heart of the Village of Partners.

———————

Upon reaching the village, Archimedes led them through a series of lanes until they reached the edge of a large town square in which there was a busy open-air marketplace. "This is a meeting ground for people preparing to ascend the peaks. Most of the basic provisions climbers need can be found here," he explained, pointing out the variety of stalls and shops.

"But to find partners, the climbers go there," he told them, calling their attention to an area far across the marketplace. There, rising behind a row of shops, stood a tall granite building topped by three domes. The trio walked across the marketplace, passed beneath a huge arched gate, continued down a long path, and entered the spacious building.

"Welcome to Partners' Common," Archimedes said.

Throughout the cavernous space, people of all ages and backgrounds gathered in pairs or small groups. Many were talking, some quite seriously and some with mirth. Others read books or studied maps together. And some simply listened and took notes on companions' thoughts and suggestions.

Beyond the Marketplace lay Partners' Common

Collectively, they were sharing information, offering support, collaborating on plans, and analyzing problems.

Partners' Common comprised three large open circular rooms that overlapped in the center, like a clover leaf. Each room's wall held a colorful mural depicting people working together in a particular way as they scaled the Four Peaks. And each mural's title was painted in flowing letters on the ceiling above it: one was entitled *Friends*; the second, *Collaborators*; and the third, *Advisers*.

Standing beneath the point where the domes met, Archimedes described the three broad categories of partners. "Friends provide social and emotional support— helping you celebrate good things, figure out complex challenges, and overcome disappointment and loss," he said. "Friendships generally begin as the most intuitive kind of relationship: you become friends with people you like and enjoy spending time with. But over time, a friend becomes a real partner when you recognize that you can trust that person and rely on him or her in adversity. And friends will always tell you the truth, even if it's a painful truth.

"Collaborators engage with you to achieve a shared goal—and in that way provide practical help. You might, for example, seek out a collaborator in a situation where each of you can only handle half the work required to achieve a goal you both want—or where you each lack necessary skills that the other possesses.

The Three-Domed
Ceiling of Partners' Common

"And advisers," Archimedes continued, "provide specialized guidance based on their own experience and the specific kinds of knowledge they possess. They will offer a lot of detailed information and share with you the lessons they've learned over time."

"I'm a little confused," Thalia said, "because I often go to my friends for advice."

Marketus added, "And my friends and I sometimes collaborate on projects for organizations we're in."

"Some longtime friends certainly can become trusted advisers, and friends with strongly shared interests can definitely become collaborators," Archimedes replied. "But the higher you climb on these peaks, the more you'll come to need partners with specialized insights. And you will find that the friends of your youth may not be able to provide those things. So you need to identify other kinds of partners who can."

Thalia nodded. "I think I get it: while an individual partner can serve more than one role, each role is distinct."

"And mixing the roles can cause problems," Marketus offered, "because a friend is not automatically an effective adviser, and a collaborator may not have what I need in a good friend."

"Precisely," Archimedes replied, then said to Thalia, "To expand on my answer to your questions this morning: parents and siblings are important; each one could also be a friend, collaborator, or adviser. But alone, they are rarely sufficient to help you handle all the challenges of Self, Work, and Community. They can provide certain kinds of information, guidance, and support. Yet they likely won't have the full array of resources and experience you will need. And, of course, family presents its own unique challenges and complications," he said with a chuckle.

Thalia took this in, then said, "So the people we see here have defined the skills and knowledge they need, then they come to Partners' Common to recruit specific partners onto their climbing teams?"

"Yes," Archimedes said.

"But how do they know whom to recruit?" Marketus asked. "Is there some kind of matching process?"

"There is no matching process," Archimedes answered. "The only practical way to find partners is to wade right in: listen to conversations, ask questions, request specific kinds of guidance, pursue suggestions—perhaps even offer some of your own skills in trade." He paused. "Why don't you both spend some time walking around the common? Talk to people who interest you and observe how folks are interacting."

Marketus and Thalia spent the next few hours individually wandering through the building, listening and watching as partnerships were created around them. When they rejoined Archimedes, Marketus had a question: "If developing partners is a continuing process, how do we go about it? We can't keep interrupting a climb to return to Partners' Common."

Archimedes replied, "As Kybernetes said, the trick is to be prepared when luck introduces you to good partners."

"In other words," Thalia said, "if we begin now to consider the kinds of people we're looking for and where we might find them, we'll get into the habit of turning our day-to-day experiences into a kind of mobile Partners' Common."

"Well put," Archimedes said. "As you traverse the peaks, each interaction can present an opportunity to create a partnership. People descending the mountain are often happy to provide advice based on their experiences. Some may offer to go back up as your collaborator in exploring a new path. And solo climbers frequently tire of ascending alone; they are eager to befriend someone with similar passions and principles."

"Is it essential that partners share our passions and principles?" Marketus asked.

"Partners must understand and respect each other's passions and principles," Archimedes replied, "and they must recognize when they conflict in a fundamental way.

Beyond that, however, the greater the range of ideas and interests your partners possess, the more they can collectively offer you."

During the ensuing week, Marketus and Thalia each undertook a series of climbs exploring the lower foothills of the Four Peaks. Before they left each morning, Archimedes reminded them to keep three questions in mind: "First, among the teams of partners you observed climbing the mountain, what role does each partner play in helping the lead climber achieve his or her goal? Second, what are the things you find particularly difficult in this climb? Third, what kinds of partners might make it easier for you?"

Thalia's and Marketus's individual hikes took them only a fraction of the way up the peaks. Nevertheless, the experiences gave them a way to compare the various challenges inherent in climbing Self, Family, Work, and Community. They took a day off between the hikes to rest their legs and discuss what they'd observed, using their Tessamarks to consider how to integrate what they were seeing and thinking. Calling up the Partners screen, they pondered the specific skills and knowledge they'd need to climb high up each peak, and using the integration capacity, they tested the ways in which their passions and principles might affect their choice of partners.

After working with his Tessamark one afternoon, Marketus told Thalia, "One thing I've learned: when I return home, I'm going to need some partners to help me think through how I want to approach Family. I grew up without parents, brothers, or sisters, so there's lots of things I don't know about the challenges of starting and being part of a family."

Thalia said, "Yeah, that makes sense. For me, I think I need to find partners who can help me pursue both Family and Work in some kind of balanced way. Because I know how important Family is, and I don't want to let that slip—but I have a strong passion, and I want to really dive into a career in engineering."

With every new hike, Thalia and Marketus became better at understanding the composition of the teams they met. Once they determined which broad role each team member played—friend, collaborator, or adviser—they could begin to see what that person offered to the lead climber.

Watching teams coming back down a mountain, they also saw evidence of what Archimedes called the law of altitude: the higher one climbs, the more important partners become and the more challenging it is to find just the right ones. "All the more reason to start identifying partners when you're young," Archimedes suggested.

Unfortunately, they also saw more than a few examples of what happens when a lead climber makes a bad choice in partners—selecting those who don't really address the lead climber's needs or who undermine the lead climber's efforts. Often, those partner mismatches were caused by a lack of clarity: the partner simply misunderstood the lead climber's goals.

Frequently, that kind of confusion occurred because the lead climber hadn't clearly thought through his or her goals—which peaks to climb, when to climb them, and how high to go—before gathering partners. Sitting outside the lodge one evening, Thalia said to Marketus, "That's what this quest is all about, isn't it? Learning how to figure out what's important to us, who's important to us, and how best to pursue our goals?"

Marketus thought for a moment, then said, "Yes, I think so."

Marketus and Thalia spent several days exploring the peaks and learning about the many ways partners could help. One morning, Archimedes said, "You've both worked hard—mentally and physically—to take in the experience these mountains offer. Perhaps it is time to continue our journey on to the next village."

Initially, the young voyagers hesitated. They had come to deeply appreciate the importance of partners and knew they had more to learn. Yet they also realized that the real work in seeking partners lay ahead, when they returned to their own lands. So the trio agreed that they would resume their journey, but not before Thalia and Marketus had a day to relax and have fun. Archimedes suggested places where they might enjoy spending the free day, and the three went off on their separate ways.

At dinner that evening, they regaled each other with their adventures in the village. Then Thalia mentioned a less-than-happy scene she'd observed: an entire team had returned, frustrated and angry, to the village just days after setting out for what was to be an extended climb of the Work peak. All had gone well initially as they hiked up the foothills that lay between the Work peak and the Family peak. But when they came to the place where the paths for Work and Family diverged, the Prime Partner—the P1, to use Xenia's term—unexpectedly turned toward Family while the lead climber remained set on reaching the top of Work. Since success on both paths demanded clear, coordinated efforts, the climb ended in disappointment for all.

"That led me to thinking about all the kinds of roles a P1 could play," Thalia said. "Should we think about the

P1 as a friend, collaborator, adviser, or some completely different category?"

Archimedes said, "In a sense, the P1 integrates the three kinds of partnerships. But Prime Partnership is much closer, emotionally and intellectually, than any other kind of alliance. It's bound by respect, love, and physical yearning. And to a much greater extent than the other three kinds of partnership, it cannot thrive without conscious commitment, mutual support, compromise, and a willingness to make sacrifices.

"Indeed, as a wise person once said, 'A happy partnership is the union of two good forgivers.' And that's a wonderful description of a successful Prime Partnership."

Archimedes added, "Never forget that your P1's passions and principles will help determine which peaks you climb and how far you ascend. The best P1s understand and accept their partners' passions and principles. And they are willing to compromise in the matter of how they pursue them."

———

The next day, before the travelers left the Village of Partners, Archimedes said, "I want to show you one other feature of Partners' Common." When they'd come to the common's gate, instead of entering the edifice,

Archimedes guided them around to a garden behind it. In its center stood a stone pedestal. He walked to it, placed his palm on its surface, and—as if it were a giant Tessamark—a sheet of light emanated from the top and displayed a long list entitled "Partnership Precepts."

Archimedes explained, "There are no formal rules for how to choose partners and how partners interact with one another. But over the years, many people have suggested precepts for forming effective partnerships based on their own experiences. The pedestal gathers and organizes all their suggestions." Then he waved his hand above the sheet of light, and the long list resolved into eight concise statements. "I have found that these eight partnership precepts offer a strong foundation for building one's team of partners."

> **BE PROACTIVE:** don't be afraid to ask people to become your partners.
>
> **EXPLAIN** clearly the role you'd like each partner to play.
>
> **DON'T ASK** partners to define your passions and principles—that's your job.
>
> **BE SURE** that your passions and principles do not conflict with your partners'.
>
> **SEEK** partners who are willing to ask hard questions and not accept easy answers.

STRIVE to make your partnerships of mutual benefit.

RECOGNIZE that each partnership will have some complications and risks.

CELEBRATE with your partners: acknowledge successes achieved and adversities overcome.

"Now place your Tessamark on the pedestal and touch the Partners Pea," Archimedes instructed. "It will record both the full list of precepts and the eight I've selected. In the future, you can use your Tessamark to consider them, develop your own, and select the precepts that you decide will work best for you."

Marketus and Thalia followed his directions, then tucked their Tessamarks into their backpacks. The trio left Partners' Common, walked back through the village, and headed onto the river trail. When the River Zoe was in sight, Archimedes observed with a chuckle, "Always remember: it takes a village to climb a mountain."

KEY IDEAS AND QUESTIONS

PARTNERS ARE ESSENTIAL: they help us take advantage of opportunities and respond to challenges effectively.

THE EARLIER IN LIFE you identify the right partners, the better prepared you are to take on complex challenges and responsibilities.

Your Prime Partner's **PASSIONS AND PRINCIPLES** will help determine which peaks you climb and how far up you go.

1. **How will you identify the kinds of knowledge, skills, and emotional strengths that you need partners to provide?**

2. **What steps have you taken to choose partners who can provide what you need?**

3. **Have you told your partners specifically what roles you'd like them to play?**

4. **Have you and your Prime Partner (or the person who might become your P1) discussed how you can help each other pursue your passions and principles?**

CHAPTER FIVE

THE VILLAGE OF PLANS 1

W hen the trio reached the river docks, they hired a small boat. On this trip, they would be both passengers and crew, so the boat's captain detailed the tasks that would be required of them. Marketus and Thalia learned quickly, and the craft soon moved out into the great Zoe.

Early on, the river flowed smoothly, and the rowing was easy. Archimedes took the opportunity to offer his insights into what lay ahead. "You have both put great energy and thought into your quests. But your ultimate success will depend not just on gathering information about your passions and principles and the partners you'll need. You must also integrate all that information into a comprehensive picture of the person you are— and the person you hope to become. That will empower you to make informed choices, not just react to events around you."

"What kinds of choices?" Thalia asked.

"First and foremost, the priorities among your passions, principles, and partners. Then the ways in which you pursue those priorities across the realms of Self, Family, Work, and Community—in other words, your *plans*," Archimedes answered.

"Those feel like pretty big choices right now," Marketus noted.

"Yes. The process of defining what's most important to you can feel overwhelming," Archimedes replied. "But keep in mind: these are not now-and-forever decisions, and there are no perfect answers. Assessing and recalibrating your priorities is a lifelong process. Even at my advanced age, I stop to consider how new experiences and knowledge affect my current priorities. So I suggest you begin by choosing two or three priorities in each realm."

He turned to Thalia. "Consider our friend Xenia, for example. When she was just a little older than you are now, she had quite a few passions: gardening, traveling, playing the cello, and studying psychology. And acting on her principles, she was very involved in several community organizations that addressed causes important to her. After great thought, weighing her principles and the input of the partners she most valued, she decided to prioritize the activities of Work and Community that allowed her to delve deeply into psychology. Eventually, those activities led her to what has become her life's work: serving as a guide to young people pursuing their quests."

"It sounds like, for Xenia, it was a process of discovery and experience—testing things that were interesting and important to her, seeing what combination might be best," Thalia said.

"Yes, I think you're right," Archimedes responded. "Xenia was testing what it might mean to pursue those activities within the world in which she lived."

Just then, the captain called their attention to a short run of white water ahead. Marketus, Thalia, and Archimedes all listened closely to his directions and concentrated on the challenge of navigating the rapids. Once they reached smooth water again, Archimedes said, "As we move along, observe the scenery around us and note its changes. Also consider the river itself: it is a metaphor for your lifelong journey. It's both challenging and ever-changing, with unexpected crosscurrents and waves. It can be confusing—a smooth surface can mask dangerous conditions beneath, while even fearsome rapids have safe channels." He paused, then said, "Ultimately, navigating this river successfully requires seeing the obvious while seeking clues to what's less visible."

Periodically over the next few hours, Thalia and Marketus had to help navigate the boat around obstacles in the river. But mostly they observed the scenery passing around them and the water flowing beneath them. At midday, their eyes were drawn to large dock on the left bank and, just beyond it, a line of red flags strung above the river.

"What are the flags for?" Thalia asked.

The captain said, "Beyond them lies a series of water-falls big enough to swamp us. So we must all work together and head straight to the dock." They did so, successfully. Then they collaborated in pulling the boat onto the riverbank. Later, the captain would hire porters to carry the boat down the path beside the falls. Where the river became navigable again, he would take on new passengers.

Archimedes, Thalia, and Marketus said goodbye and set off on a path that rose steadily away from the river-bank. After an hour's walk, they found themselves over-looking the Zoe from hundreds of feet above, the river valley stretching out for miles.

"Wow," Thalia said. "You can almost see forever."

"Indeed. But the view is even more interesting from the village," Archimedes assured her, and the trio resumed walking.

Their path curved away from the river toward a series of broad plateaus that rolled out in four gentle waves, each rising higher than the one before it. Those plateaus, Archimedes explained, held the Village of Plans. The village community—its homes, shops, social halls, and lodges—covered the first plateau. The other three each held a single structure. Archimedes guided

Marketus and Thalia toward the first, where they would find a lodge and their evening meal. As they walked, Marketus asked, "What are those three buildings?"

"We will explore them tomorrow," Archimedes replied. "The first will enable you to understand the context in which you will pursue your life's *priorities*—the environment in which you will live and the factors that will drive change within it. The second will help you identify the *opportunities* your environment offers for pursuing your passions and principles and finding your partners. In the third building, you will choose which opportunities to pursue and then map out paths toward them."

The next day, they walked up to the building on the village's second plateau, a tall circular structure with no windows and just a single door at its base. The building was surrounded by a series of gardens, each filled with a wide variety of flowers, bushes, and trees. Archimedes led them toward the building's entrance, where a woman stood waiting. She had a regal bearing but smiled warmly as they approached.

Archimedes bowed to the woman, then said, "Thalia and Marketus, this is Arianne, Chief Mentor in the Village of Plans."

"Welcome, voyagers. We are honored by your visit," Arianne said. Beckoning toward a garden bench, she said, "Please, sit for a few moments and tell me about yourselves."

Marketus and Thalia told her about their backgrounds and described the most significant experiences of their quests. Arianne listened carefully, then said, "Excellent. During the next few weeks, I think you will make good use of our knowledge and expertise." Then, turning to Archimedes, she said, "The final pea?"

He took from his satchel two small silk bags tied with crimson cords. Without prompting, Marketus and Thalia took out their Tessamarks and placed the Planning Peas in their devices.

"You have started the process of defining yourselves and prioritizing your passions, principles, and potential partners," Arianne said. "In this village, you will clarify those priorities and ultimately make plans about how to act on them. First, though, you must answer two questions: How will my passions and principles fit in with the environment I will inhabit? And what opportunities will that environment offer for pursuing them successfully?"

Gesturing to the building, she said, "This is the Environment Exploratorium. It will help you understand the environment around you. In particular, it will shed light on how the environment changes and what opportunities those changes create."

Archimedes spoke up. "You will recall that yesterday I asked you to observe the river as we traveled over it. The ancient Greek author Heraclitus once said, 'No man ever steps in the same river twice, for it's not the same river and he's not the same man.' Heraclitus meant that change is constant for us and our environment.

"That fact may not be obvious at first. But if you observe carefully, you can note how the environment changes and why."

"Why is observing change important?" Thalia asked.

"Observing change enables you to understand your environment as it actually is—not as it may once have been—and how it came to be that way," Arianne responded.

"In other words," Marketus suggested, "observing change involves both tracking the path that brought us to the place where we are now and watching history unfold in real time."

"Yes, exactly," Arianne replied. "It offers one other benefit as well: tracking the path of change as it occurs helps you anticipate the impact it will have on your future. That is important information to have when you're choosing the most effective paths to take in your life's journey."

With that, Arianne ushered the two voyagers into the building. Archimedes, knowing there was no role for him in the exploratorium, went to spend some contemplative time in the gardens.

Inside, the building was mostly dark. The only light emanated from two hollow glass columns, each twenty feet around. When their eyes adjusted, Marketus and Thalia realized that the back-to-back columns rose from the floor to the ceiling of a vast room.

At Arianne's direction, Thalia walked through an entryway in one of the glass columns, and Marketus walked through an entryway in the other. They sat at small control panels facing opposite sides of the building. And then the room filled with light from video screens covering the walls.

"The exploratorium is an immersive experience offering sights, sounds, and written information about the environment you come from," Arianne explained. "It has two purposes: to help you understand how your environment came to be as it is now and to help you anticipate what it will be like in the future. To do that, the exploratorium will introduce you to what we call change drivers—the major forces that shape the way an environment evolves over time.

"There are many change drivers operating simultaneously in every environment. But the four primary change drivers are Economics, Government, Demographics, and Technology. When you slide your Tessamark into the cradle on your control panel, the exploratorium will

enable you to experience virtually how each of the four primary drivers operates in your environment.

"Your explorations will start on this level, with Economics. When you have absorbed as much information as you can, simply push the Next button on the control panel, and the platform on which you are sitting will be raised to the next section—Government—then Demographics, then Technology. Once you've been introduced to all four, you can push the button for a specific driver and go directly there. That way you can consider questions and ideas as they occur to you.

"Move at your own pace. When you're ready for a break, just push the Exit button, and the platform will return to this level and illuminate the door to the gardens outside."

Looking up toward the faraway ceiling, Marketus said, "There seem to be a lot more than four levels."

"There are indeed," Arianne replied. "Most of our visitors find that the four primary change drivers are more than enough to take in. But if you are so inclined, you can also explore change drivers such as Geography, Culture, Public Health, Religion, and many others."

With that, Arianne instructed Marketus and Thalia to place their Tessamarks in their control panels, and the immersions began.

––––––––––

Over the course of the following week, the voyagers engaged with the exploratorium in different ways. Thalia was methodical, exploring each environmental driver as deeply as possible before moving on to the next. Marketus moved between environmental drivers as his curiosity dictated; most days, he interacted with all four primary drivers. However, he ended up spending the most time with the Economics driver. And Thalia spent the most time with the Technology driver.

Overall, they found the exploratorium immersion both amazing and scary. They enjoyed learning new things about their environments. Yet they were humbled by how much they'd not previously realized about the world around them. That feeling only grew when, at dinner one night, Archimedes said, "You have made a good start in exploring the drivers of your environments. What can you tell me about how the drivers evolved—what their histories are?" Marketus and Thalia could only answer his question in bits and pieces.

"History is a powerful tool," Archimedes observed. "The way that today's environmental drivers evolved is often a clue to how they will operate in the future. Those clues improve your ability to predict how your priorities will fit the environment as it changes and what opportunities there may be."

Heeding Archimedes's words, Thalia and Marketus each spent several days in the exploratorium focusing on the histories of the four main environmental drivers. And one morning, Arianne joined them. "Archimedes tells me you have worked hard to understand the evolution of your environments," she said. "I wonder: Did you notice any patterns to the changes?"

Thalia said, "I saw no overall pattern in the speed of change. Demographics-driven change moves slowly, but Technology-driven change is often pretty fast."

"I noticed a lot of peaks and valleys, especially with Economics-driven change," Marketus observed.

Arianne walked over to one of the control panels and typed a phrase into the keyboard. The exploratorium's screens lit up, displaying a variety of wavy lines. "You are both correct," she said. "The speed, nature, and focus of change are all variable. But there is one consistent pattern of change: we call it an S Curve. S Curves are dynamic, ongoing cycles made up of a series of waves: each has a bottom, an upswing, a crest, and a decline to the next bottom." She gestured to the screens. "The curves are not always smooth; some have small peaks and valleys within the larger waves, and some are packed closely together. But the general pattern is the same."

At Arianne's suggestion, Marketus and Thalia took their seats at the control panels, placed their Tessamarks in the cradles, and typed in "S Curves." The exploratorium immediately immersed them in S Curves from

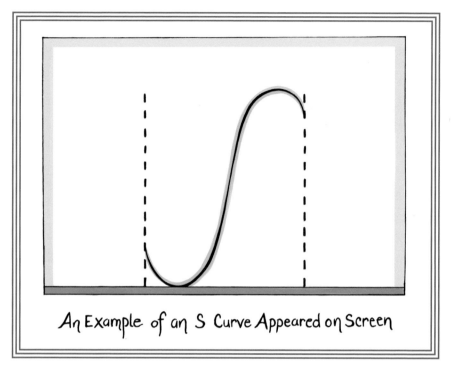

An Example of an S Curve Appeared on Screen

their environments. Some described the flow of change within historical periods, such as the rise and fall of empires. Others described waves still flowing, such as the continual changes in fashion and music.

———

Thalia and Marketus left the exploratorium at the end of that day feeling like they'd stepped off a long roller-coaster ride. When Arianne joined them and Archimedes at dinner that evening, Marketus was still wrestling with the concept of S Curves and their relevance. "I understand how S Curves reflect the changes around us," he said.

"But I don't see how they fit in with my choice of priorities and how I will pursue them. Why does it matter if we're at the top or bottom of an S Curve?"

Arianne understood his confusion. "Let's consider a very basic S Curve you both have observed: the growth of crops in the fields. If you're a farmer, the amount you harvest depends a lot on when you plant your seeds. Plant in the spring, and you will be able to take advantage of a long period of sun and warmth in which to grow your crop. Plant in midsummer, and you have only half the time to take advantage of ideal conditions before cooler, shorter days set in, so your crop is less productive."

Marketus said, "But most of the S Curves I observed in the exploratorium were not simple annual cycles. And besides," he joked, "farming is definitely not one of my passions."

"No indeed," Archimedes replied with a smile. "So here's a more complex example—one that may resonate with your enjoyment of music. In your land, not long before you were born, many people listened to music played on compact discs, and they purchased these CDs from a physical store. For twenty years or more, the S Curve for CDs was rising, and people could earn a very good living by manufacturing blank CDs or by selling them. Eventually, though, different ways of acquiring music—downloading and streaming—were developed. And the S Curve for CDs began falling."

"Meaning that as the number of people who purchased CDs declined, it became much harder for musicians, manufacturers, and retailers to earn a living from them—even if they were really passionate about music, right?" Marketus asked.

"That's right," Archimedes said.

Thalia thought about the examples a bit, then said, "So in practical terms, catching a rising curve means that you need much less effort to succeed. It's like the difference between riding a bike with the wind at your back or in your face."

"Yes, exactly," Arianne said.

"But how do you catch a wave at just the right time?"

"It can be difficult to know exactly where a cycle stands at any point," Arianne acknowledged. "And it is complicated by the fact that it's human nature to believe that the current situation—whether good or bad—will continue indefinitely, even though it almost never does. Still, making a good, objective guess of where you are on the curve will help you assess what to prioritize and what opportunities to pursue."

Archimedes spoke up. "Arianne, may I offer two cautionary points? First, S Curves are important, but they should not outweigh all other considerations. If you have a high-priority passion, and pursuing it gives you great joy and energy—regardless of the outcome—perhaps you should overlook the fact that there is a declining wave. Second, remember that creative, energetic, and determined people can create opportunities that counter the general flow of the curve. In some cases, they even jump-start a whole new S Curve, which is what inventors, innovators, and entrepreneurs often do."

"But what happens if the opposite is true—I see a rising S Curve that fits one of my low-priority passions?" Marketus asked.

"Then you have choices to make," Arianne replied. "Some people choose to catch that rising wave because it will enable them to pursue several secondary priorities simultaneously rather than a single top priority. Or because it positions them to effectively pursue that top priority down the road."

Arianne let those ideas sink in, then said, "Often, these are not ideal, fun, or simple choices. But they are challenges you should be ready to deal with.

"In fact," she added, "you will begin to grapple with them tomorrow, when you go to the next plateau and enter the Integration Matrix."

KEY IDEAS AND QUESTIONS

UNDERSTANDING YOUR ENVIRONMENT is essential to creating an effective life plan.

OBSERVING CHANGE enables you to understand how your environment came to be as it is, see how it may change, and anticipate how it may affect your future.

CATCHING THE RISING WAVE of an S Curve is often a powerful and relatively easy way to pursue your passions and principles.

1. **How well do your passions and principles fit with your environment?**

2. **What opportunities for pursuing your most important passions and principles are available in your environment?**

3. **In what ways are Economics, Government, Demographics, and Technology driving change in your environment?**

4. **Are there other significant change drivers affecting your environment?**

5. **What are some of the S Curves operating in your environment?**

CHAPTER SIX

THE VILLAGE OF PLANS 2

The Integration Matrix was housed in a square building twenty feet high and sixty feet wide on each side.

Its four walls were made of thick opaque glass. To enter, Arianne led Thalia and Marketus down a stairway that passed beneath the east wall then back up into the structure. Inside, there were two large rectangular rooms separated by a wall of dark glass. Each room was empty save for a small illuminated control panel and chair. It was a deceptively simple environment, given what could be accomplished there.

"One of the biggest challenges you face is evaluating all the information you've gathered," Arianne began. "How do you make sense of the many ways that passions, principles, realms, environments, and change drivers might intersect? How do you evaluate the resulting opportunities and choose what to prioritize? The Integration Matrix helps you organize your information and thoughts into concrete options. Then it creates scenarios for ways in which they may play out."

The Integration Matrix was a sophisticated holographic system guided by data in the Tessamark and instructions spoken by its owner. From this information, it could build fully interactive three-dimensional holographic experiences. It could also create intricate maps and data analyses and adapt them in every way imaginable.

Thalia and Marketus had some difficulty learning the system's operations. But once they did, they found the experience exhilarating. They could put together any combination of priorities drawn from their passions, principles, and partners in every realm, observe relevant S Curves at work, and project the results of their choices.

At that night's dinner, they could hardly stop talking about the dozens of combinations they investigated. "I'm glad you found it fun and that you've identified so many opportunities," Archimedes said. "But now it's time for the challenging part: whittling down your options."

"Yeah, I was waiting for the other shoe to drop," Thalia responded wryly.

"To take this next step," Arianne instructed them, "you must provide the Integration Matrix with two more kinds of information. We call them balance factors.

"The first balance factor is your Time and Energy Allocation. Because supplies of time and energy are limited, you must make decisions about how much of them you want to spend on each priority in each realm. The Time and Energy Allocation comes into play when, for example, an otherwise ideal opportunity in the Work realm leaves less time than you want for Self and Community. It helps you understand the cost of pursuing one opportunity at the expense of another."

"I detect a theme here," Marketus said. "Tough choices."

Archimedes nodded. "You will encounter tough choices throughout your life. But your choices will be most effective when you bring lots of information into the decision-making process. And the process will become less anxiety-producing the more you practice making conscious, thoughtful choices."

"Rather than letting fate—or other people—make choices for you," Thalia said.

"Exactly," Archimedes replied.

Arianne let those thoughts sink in. Then she explained the second balance factor. "I call it the Money-Achievement-Happiness Calculation. In simple terms, how will you balance your efforts to make money, achieve personal goals, and simply enjoy life? And how will that balance play out in each realm?"

"Shouldn't the answers simply be reflections of our passions and principles—and the goals of our P1s?" asked Marketus.

LESSON:

Your choices will be most effective when **YOU BRING LOTS OF INFORMATION** into the decision-making process and are truly honest with yourself.

Arianne replied, "Yes, but there's nothing simple about it. First, because as your passions, principles, and partners evolve, so, too, should your Money-Achievement-Happiness Calculation.

"Second—and this is very important—the calculation is a way of incorporating your financial, intellectual, and emotional needs into the process of allocating your time and energy. For that reason, you must be very honest with yourself about what's 'enough' . . . enough money, enough achievement, and enough happiness. Then you can make the choices—the trade-offs of time and energy—that are necessary to have enough of each."

Marketus and Thalia were quiet for a bit while they considered the two new factors. Then Arianne said, "During your last few days in the Integration Matrix, think deeply about these balance factors and their implications. You do not need to make definitive choices yet about your priorities and the opportunities you'll pursue. Just settle on a handful of options that feel good. Once you've done so, press the Planning Pea to record them in your Tessamark."

"At that point," Archimedes noted, "you will be ready to move on to the Planning Studio. There you will experience the culmination of your quest."

At Work in the Planning Studio

Three mornings later, the quartet walked up to the Planning Studio. The building, standing on the highest plateau, rose up on four tall marble pillars and afforded a panoramic view of the river valley and the surrounding mountains. The structure's exterior was made of clear glass, each pane set at a slightly different angle from those around it. From the outside, the Planning Studio looked like a giant multifaceted diamond.

Leading them inside the building, Arianne revealed to Thalia and Marketus the task that lay before them. "From all your previous work, you have a sense of the priorities you may choose from and the best opportunities for putting them into practice. Now you must determine which priorities to pursue and which paths to take."

Arianne led them up a long flight of stairs to an open sunlit room filled with drafting tables. She motioned them toward two unoccupied tables, beside which sat stacks of paper and boxes of pencils and drafting tools. "Here you will create your individual Life-Plan Maps," she said.

Marketus looked perplexed as he examined his table. Anticipating his question, Archimedes smiled and said, "Sorry—no electronic devices here. The Environment Exploratorium and Integration Matrix helped you synthesize all the information you gathered in the first three villages. Your Tessamark now holds those syntheses; by all means use it. But the tool you most need to rely on now is here," he said, tapping Marketus lightly on the forehead. "It is time for making choices and determining how to act on them."

Arianne picked up a sheet of paper and a pencil. "A Life-Plan Map must reflect the interplay of three things," she said, then wrote the following list.

1. A PERSON'S PASSIONS, PRINCIPLES, AND PARTNERS and the way they are prioritized

2. A PERSON'S ENVIRONMENT and the opportunities it presents in each realm

3. THE ACTIONS that a person will take to pursue those opportunities

"But more simply," she went on, "your Life-Plan Map is the answer to a straightforward question: What series of actions will I take to most effectively match who I am with my environment and the opportunities it offers?"

"So," Thalia said, "on the Life-Plan Map, our actions will determine our path forward. That seems pretty concrete and straightforward."

"Yes, concrete, but not set in stone—if you'll excuse the pun," Arianne responded. "The river of life is ever-changing. So your Life-Plan Maps must be living documents. They should evolve over time, based on the outcomes of your actions and what you learn from them."

―――――――

At the outset, the task of drafting the Life-Plan Maps proved challenging. The work stretched over many days and a few late nights. Thalia and Marketus each made several false starts. This frustrated them, but Arianne offered reassurance. "Understanding what won't work is almost as important as finding out what will," she said.

She also suggested that they speak with other mapmakers working in the Planning Studio. "Some, like you, are drafting their first Life-Plan Maps and find it difficult," Arianne noted. "The rest are updating maps and would be happy to offer guidance." Marketus and Thalia kept at the task, buoyed by their interactions with the other mapmakers.

One afternoon, Archimedes came to the Planning Studio and said, "Let's take a break from your labors. The village's Festival of Chance has begun. You'll enjoy it."

On the slopes between the four plateaus, colorful tents offered games of chance and games of skill. Everyone in the village—residents and visitors alike—participated in the games, which were a welcome change from the intensive planning that was the focus of the village's daily work.

"Let's try our luck," Archimedes said. "Above all else, let's have fun." And they did. Thalia and Marketus came away with a few trinkets from the games they'd won. Archimedes's luck wasn't as good, but it had not lessened his enjoyment.

That evening, they sat in one of the exploratorium's gardens, happily munching popped corn, candied fruits, and other treats. "This was great," Thalia said between crunches, "and completely unexpected in a place as serious as this."

Archimedes replied, "It is fun with the serious purpose of reminding us of two things. First, you cannot plan for the impact of luck, good and bad. You can only be flexible in responding to it.

"Second, you should acknowledge the fact that there are situations beyond your control: admit when success results from good luck, not just from your efforts and abilities, and give yourself a break when setbacks come from bad luck or unfortunate circumstances, not your actions or shortcomings.

"As a young person, I had a long string of bad luck," Archimedes recalled. "Since then, I have had wonderful luck in finding great partners and fruitful opportunities. Of course, it helped that I was prepared to respond to the partners and opportunities that luck brought me."

After a good deal of work, Marketus and Thalia each had a complete and well-drawn Life-Plan Map. With a sense of accomplishment, they presented them for Arianne's review. She considered each map in detail, then smiled broadly and said, "You have both fulfilled your quests. These maps should give you confidence about the paths you will travel when you return to your lands."

The next morning, it was time to leave the Village of Plans. As the two voyagers and their guide were preparing to travel, Arianne came to their lodge. "You will want to preserve your Life-Plan Maps in good condition," she said, "so I've brought you a parting gift." She handed Thalia and Marketus each a hollow wooden cylinder with beautifully carved images of rivers running in gentle S patterns. The ends of the cylinder were covered by wooden caps with pea tendrils etched into them. "Roll your maps inside these, and they will be protected from all manner of things."

Then Arianne offered her parting thoughts. "Keep your Life-Plan Maps current, reflecting your progress and the changes taking place around you. Indeed, seek out change. Study it. Anticipate it. Where possible, create it and take advantage of it. And never be afraid to test new paths."

With that, Arianne bowed and bade them farewell.

An hour later, Archimedes led Marketus and Thalia out of the village, retracing the path from the river. Then they followed the trail running beside the falls until they reached the place where the water was calm. A small raft and its captain awaited, ready to take Thalia and Marketus downriver. Where the Zoe widened into a delta and met the ocean, they would find boats waiting to carry them back to their respective homelands.

Knowing that parting from Archimedes would be difficult, Marketus and Thalia had said their formal goodbyes the night before. They'd both expressed their great appreciation, and he expressed his pride in their accomplishments. He assured them that they would be welcome to visit the four villages in the future. And he reminded them to continue employing their Tessamarks. "The device will only become more useful over time, and you will have many occasions to refer back to it."

At the riverside, Thalia and Marketus both made a low, formal bow to Archimedes, then climbed into the raft. Taking up their paddles, they turned to look ahead—ready to begin another, much longer journey.

KEY IDEAS AND QUESTIONS

TIME AND ENERGY ARE LIMITED, and we must allocate them carefully among our priorities in each of the four realms.

It's important to draw up a **MONEY-ACHIEVEMENT-HAPPINESS CALCULATION** and consider its effect on your priorities and plans.

YOU CANNOT PLAN FOR LUCK: you can only be flexible in responding to it and recognize its impact, good and bad.

1. How are you presently allocating time and energy among Self, Family, Work, and Community?

2. How might that allocation change?

3. How do you currently balance making money, achieving personal goals, and just enjoying life?

4. How might that balance change?

5. Can you identify times in your life when a positive result came as much from good luck as from your efforts and abilities?

6. How about times when a setback resulted as much from bad luck or unfortunate circumstances as from your actions or shortcomings?

The Journey Through the Four Villages

The Village of Plans

Waterfall

The Four Peaks

The Village of Partners

The Village of Principles

The River Zoe

The Village of Passions

CODA

Several decades later, Marketus once again stood on the beach observing the forests and mountains of the amazing land he had first traveled through so long ago. In many ways, the view appeared as it did when he was a young man. Yet it was different, for he knew the insights and experiences that were to be found in the villages, valleys, and peaks beyond the beach.

Of course, he was different, too. He had the knowledge born of actively following the paths laid out on his Life-Plan Map, based on his passions and principles. He had the experience of joining with partners to pursue the opportunities life presented and those he had created for himself. He also had wisdom born of success and failure.

Marketus had been lucky. The good outcomes had far outweighed the bad outcomes in his life. He had caught several rising waves on the S Curves he encountered. But he'd also been prepared for what luck had brought. The Life-Plan Map he created here had proved an excellent foundation for responding to the changes he found in himself and in the world around him.

Marketus had returned frequently to this land. Early on, he came back to refresh his sense of himself and his plans; each time, he left with an updated map secured in his cherished wooden cylinder. In recent years, he had accompanied Archimedes as a partner-guide. Today was different, however, and he was nervous: this would be his first trip as a solo guide.

He watched as a small boat ran up on the beach.

A young man hopped out, settled a backpack on his shoulders, and surveyed the forest before him. When the boat slowly moved away, the young man waved goodbye, then walked up the beach toward Marketus.

"Welcome," Marketus said.

The young voyager asked, "Are you the person who will be my guide?"

"I'm the person who will show you how to become your own guide," Marketus replied with a broad smile. "Let us begin the journey."

The END...
and the BEGINNING

PART II

Behind the Fable

A CHALLENGING JOURNEY

Now, briefly, another story. But this one is absolutely true.

The 1930s were a tough time for a lot of people, including a man named Jack. Once a successful self-made New York businessman, he was left at rock bottom by the stock market crash and the Depression—financially bankrupt and psychologically broken.

So, in 1933, he threw a suitcase in his car and headed west to make a brand-new start. In Saint Louis, Jack met a beautiful eighteen-year-old woman, Sophie. They instantly fell in love, married just a few weeks later, and together headed to California.

Unfortunately, the new location didn't lead to new job prospects for Jack. He was frequently without work, and the couple struggled financially. Their one consolation was the birth of their son, Eddie. But when the joy of new parenthood wore off, the reality of having a child to feed weighed heavily on Jack. He desperately sought work wherever it could be found as the family traveled across country, from the Mojave Desert to Georgia to wherever else opportunities arose. The jobs rarely lasted long, though: Jack's inflexible personality led him into conflict with boss after boss.

By 1939, it all became too much for Sophie. She divorced Jack, gained custody of their three-year-old son, and returned to Saint Louis to live with her family. Jack had visiting rights on Sundays but was never able to see his son, because he remained in Los Angeles, a twenty-six-hour drive away. But one Sunday, he made the long trip to Saint Louis and picked up the boy for a scheduled visit. He told Sophie they were going to lunch and a movie. In fact, Jack headed onto Route 66 and back to Los Angeles. He called Sophie from a rest stop and told her he was taking their son, and he warned her not to look for them—or *else*. Feeling threatened by Jack, she never commenced the search.

For two years, father and son lived in a series of cheap hotels around Los Angeles. When Jack finally found steady work as a radio operator aboard a merchant ship, he left Eddie with neighbors. From time to time, when Jack came back to town, he and Eddie shared a boys' paradise of beach trips, movies, walks through the city, and jaunts along the docks.

By late 1941, Jack was back on track to financial success. Through hard work and frugal living, he'd saved enough money to buy several small tuna-fishing boats and hire experienced Japanese immigrant fishermen. His five-year-old son spent many pleasant days at sea, enjoying the water and watching the crew haul in nets filled with fish. The experiences helped the boy overcome the sadness of knowing that his mother had died—which is what Jack had told him.

That December, the father-son idyll ended with the bombing of Pearl Harbor. In a matter of weeks, Jack's all-Japanese crews were sent to heavily guarded camps, and his business fell apart. Soon after, Jack went to sea as a commissioned officer in the US Merchant Marine. He told the boy he'd been called into the service because of his experience as a radio operator. But few forty-one-year-old single parents were being drafted. More likely, Jack had enlisted—fleeing another heartbreaking financial setback, seeing no other way to support his son.

During the next five years, father and son didn't see each other at all. Put in foster care, the boy lived with five different families, who ranged from cold and abusive to warm and caring. During these years, Eddie never saw his dad. Still, the boy was buoyed by some important personal characteristics of his own: he was intelligent, sociable, and had lots of energy. He did well in school, played many sports, and worked after school and during the summers. He also had a strong sense of self-worth, because whatever Jack's faults were, he always expressed confidence in his boy's abilities.

In 1946, Jack was discharged from the Merchant Marine and arranged for his ten-year old son to fly across the country, alone, to meet him in New York. During the ensuing year, father and son lived in a New York YMCA and then in a Coney Island hotel.

The boy went to a local school and did well. But Jack could not find a job and grew increasingly despondent. Finally, he took the only path available to him—returning to the sea as a radio operator on a merchant vessel. Jack worked hard to find a local family his son could live with, but at the last minute, the arrangements fell through.

And so the boy was on his own for a month—living in a Coney Island hotel room, eating at a nearby deli, and taking the subway into Manhattan each day to explore the city. Jack had paid the hotel and deli in advance. But beyond that, the boy was left to care for himself, guided by a mixture of fear, common sense, and self-reliance. At summer's end, still with no foster family available, he was admitted to an orphanage in Coney Island.

The boy worried quite a bit about what the orphanage would be like. But after a not-so-simple rite of passage, Eddie adjusted quickly and actually found it a positive experience. In fact, the orphanage turned out to be an unexpected lucky break for him because he finally found two things he'd never had: *community* and *consistency.*

The orphanage also gave his life a *structure* that it never had before. Life with his father, and life on his own, had been almost free-form; he rarely knew what to expect. But now, he took comfort in the routines of the institution.

Everyone slept in one large room, ate meals together at long tables, and attended the same school. For the first time, he developed lasting friendships and was able to demonstrate his natural leadership skills. Just as important, he could focus on school in a sustained way, with diligence and intelligence. He lived in that orphanage for three years, getting letters and occasional visits from Jack.

Then, in mid-1950, Jack simply disappeared. As a result, the boy was declared a ward of New York State, and soon he was transferred to another orphanage. Initially, the transition was tough, but the boy was getting to be an expert in managing change. He figured out how to take advantage of all the academic, athletic, and social opportunities the new place offered. Eventually, Jack resurfaced, but he never again played a central role in his son's life. He didn't even come to Eddie's high school graduation. The self-sufficient boy stood there alone, understanding that he had to be responsible for himself and take control of his destiny.

At seventeen, he made a life-changing decision: he would find a way to go to a private college, even if he didn't have the money to pay for it. That may seem an obvious step for a smart kid today, but back then—especially for someone who was essentially an orphan with no money—it was a path filled with risk and uncertainty. But the boy made it work. He won a Navy ROTC scholarship and was accepted at the University of Rochester.

Arriving on the campus for the first time, he felt a sense of opportunity and rebirth. He would no longer be known as a parentless, penniless child; he would no longer be dependent on the people around him. He would simply be an energetic, smart guy determined to make friends and succeed in life. Once he got to the campus, he locked his past in a dark closet and never spoke of his origins.

He also set out to make sure he would never again be without the three things that were most important to him: a loving family, a secure home, and absolute financial security.

Of course, it wasn't a simple process. He had to work very hard, and sometimes he struggled with depression and powerful anger—the delayed reactions to his childhood experiences of abandonment and uncertainty. But he won those struggles, powered by a belief that he could attain his goals if he kept moving toward them.

He graduated from college, served three years as a naval officer, worked as an engineer, then went to Harvard Business School. He married a wonderful woman and raised three children with her, and built a very successful business career. And over the years, he endowed more than two hundred scholarships for students who, like him, needed help to pay for their education.

While generally successful, those decades were certainly not carefree. There were plenty of challenges and setbacks, times of uncertainty and frustration. But the man had learned much from his difficult boyhood years, and he used those lessons to overcome the hurdles and reversals he experienced as an adult.

There is one more episode to this story. In 1996, the son came across a battered suitcase filled with old letters and documents; it had been sitting in a closet, forgotten and unopened, since Jack's death, decades before. Reading the brittle, yellowed papers, the son made an amazing discovery: his mother had not died in 1939, as Jack had told him. The son immediately undertook a search and found that Sophie was still alive and well at the age of eighty-one. He reached out to her, and for the following twelve years—until she died, at the age of ninety-three—they were a family again.

Of course, I am Jack and Sophie Hajim's son.

PLANNING AND TRANSFORMING

Though my early experiences may have been somewhat unique, I'm not alone in having felt loss, disappointment, fear, and uncertainty about my path in life. Most of us have had these experiences to one degree or another. And I have no doubt that you will face many of the same kinds of challenges I've faced through my adult years—how to succeed at work, how to be part of a family, how to contribute to your community, and how to consistently feel positive about yourself.

In *The Island of the Four Ps*, I have tried to capture the important lessons I've gleaned from both my difficult early years and the subsequent decades, which have been successful but challenging in their own way.

Until I was eighteen, my life felt like a game of dice that was rigged against me. Hard experience showed me the value of taking control of my life. And it taught me that taking control requires (1) figuring out how to plan, (2) creating a plan, and (3) pursuing that plan with determination.

So using a pencil and pad of paper—the iPad of my youth—I started writing down both my goals and the problems I wanted to overcome. I'd list thoughts, ideas, and concerns; identify pros and cons of various options; note my conclusions; then list specific action steps and ways to measure my progress. And I've continued doing that throughout my life. My real iPad get lots of use these days, but I still do most of my life-thinking on paper.

You can't subcontract the life-thinking process. You can't just google "my road map to happiness and success" to find your life plan. You have to get your thoughts and ideas down in concrete terms so you can examine them, consider all the what-ifs, and set specific action steps toward your goals. In *The Island of the Four Ps*, the Tessamark symbolizes this process. It joins the physical act of recording information and ideas with the intellectual and emotional processing that can only be done in our minds.

Thinking effectively about your future—who you want to be, where you want to go, what you want to achieve, and what will make you happy—can be difficult, even frustrating. It helps to have guidance from people who have traveled before you. That's why I read lots of books of all kinds. They help me understand the world around me. Often, they help me better understand myself.

Malcolm Gladwell's book *David and Goliath* examines the advantages of *disadvantages*—the idea that certain kinds of adversity can be beneficial. Experiencing disadvantages,

Gladwell suggests, can make a person emotionally strong, resilient, and able to accomplish ambitious goals. I would add that they can also help a person use and build upon the advantages that he or she *does* have.

My childhood and teenage years were pretty bleak. No settled home, no consistent parenting, little financial support. Despite the adversity, I did have two advantages. First was my father's strong emotional support. True, he abandoned me at important times. But whether in person or through letters, he always conveyed his unconditional love for me. He always expressed confidence in my abilities. He "knew" I was destined for better things than he could provide. Dad's emotional support was a constant that buoyed my self-confidence throughout my life.

My second advantage was a strong passion for science and math. It enabled me to catch the rising science and technology wave that carried me through college, my first job, and into Harvard Business School. Later, I was able to apply my knowledge of science and math in the world of investing, where I caught another rising wave, which led me to financial success.

Just as important, however, were the disadvantages that I transformed into advantages. When I was a child, there was often no one around to help me; self-reliance was the only way to survive. I became comfortable with independence—with overcoming difficult situations by myself and making tough choices. I became confident that I could handle almost any challenge. In other words, the disadvantages of abandonment became the advantages of autonomy, decisiveness, and optimism.

Growing up, I was often lonely. But this disadvantage was transformed once I got to college, where I used years of childhood loneliness as a kind of emotional fuel. I deliberately surrounded myself with people, joined organizations, and took on leadership roles. Beyond developing enduring friendships, I gained priceless experience in being part of a team, working within organizations, and being a leader. Another disadvantage turned into an advantage.

One of my biggest childhood disadvantages was a nearly complete lack of control over my day-to-day life. Almost anything—good or bad—could be coming down the road at me, so I had to pay close attention to my environment. I needed to understand how things worked and to recognize the signals of change. As a result, I got very good at looking ahead, spinning out scenarios, and uncovering clues. Among other benefits, this helped me develop the ability to pick good financial investments. The disadvantage-turned-advantage of paying attention to the environment helped me earn a good living.

We all have inherent advantages. And all of us have the capacity to positively transform at least some of our disadvantages into advantages. When we knit together our inherent and "transformed" advantages—and add a dash of good luck—each of us can accomplish wonderful things.

At the same time, knowing that something is possible isn't the same as knowing exactly how to make it a reality. As a result, we all have false starts; they're unavoidable. But there are ways to minimize the negative impact of those false starts. Paying close attention to our passions, principles, partners, and plans helps us do just that.

PASSIONS

I was in my twenties before I realized that I had two passions even more significant than science and math: making organizations work and helping people achieve more than they thought they could. My successes in the Work and Community realms have come from uniting those passions with my inherent and acquired advantages.

Like me, many people need to dig a bit to uncover their most important passions. They need to see them in action to recognize them. That is why it's important to be open to new experiences, which can uncover your passions. While some of those experiences will come to naught, you should consider them a good investment—because knowing what paths not to pursue frees time and energy, allowing you to follow more fruitful paths.

Sometimes our passions can overwhelm us with the energy they create. It is important to recognize when and how we are being driven by "unproductive" passions. We all have them, to one extent or another, and they fall along a broad spectrum. For example, my passion for financial security, which drove me to work very hard, was generally productive. At times, however, it became much too strong and stole time and energy that I had promised to my family. It's important that, whenever possible, we recognize our unproductive passions and develop ways of channeling them in constructive ways. The best way to do that is by bringing the other Ps to bear: lay out the principles that will guide your decisions and actions, make clear plans that you can fall back on in moments of confusion, and seek partners who can help you wrestle with the challenges.

PRINCIPLES

Without principles to direct them, even the most constructive passions can become unproductive or dangerous. By helping guide your conduct, principles shape (and, if necessary, moderate) your passion-driven energy and determination. They provide a useful structure and organization to your life and are essential elements of an effective plan.

We derive our principles from many places—family, community, education, religion, and life experience. When first contemplating their principles, many people are like Marketus: they follow a few informal rules, but they rarely connect those rules directly with their basic beliefs. In our 24-7, 365 culture, it's easy to accept ideas and rules without deeply considering them. But avoiding that consideration is dangerous, emotionally and morally, especially if we're adopting someone else's values simply because we admire that person or aspire to be like him or her in one way or another.

It's also a problem to absorb the principles of organizations we belong to without measuring their fit for us as individuals. You cannot plan effectively for your future without having taken the time to contemplate your own principles and how you will live them out. And your plan gets stale if you don't continue to examine your principles in light of new experiences and insights.

The principles that Archimedes wrote down for Marketus are my own.

> **TREAT** others as you hope to be treated.
>
> **SEEK** freedom to make your own decisions.
>
> **DECIDE** what's enough—enough money, possessions, accomplishments, recognition, engagement, and love—and don't pursue more than enough.

These principles reflect the many kinds of experiences I've had, both as a child and as a working adult. They also reflect the wide reading I've done, my close study of the ways in which the people around me applied principles to their own lives, and the guidance I've received from many highly principled partners. I've combed through all that experience and consciously chosen principles for what they mean to me. I've discarded many other possibilities—even those that are hugely important to people I respect—because they don't fit who I truly am. Knowing that these principles are indeed my own, I confidently use them to guide my important decisions and my interactions with people around me.

Strive to define your own set of principles, one at a time. Pay attention to how you act on them, and be honest about why you conduct yourself as you do. Recognize how the changes in your life reflect—or should be reflected in—your principles.

PARTNERS

Having spent much of my childhood without partners, I've embraced them as an adult. But you don't have to be parentless to find great benefit in partners. No individual can succeed alone. With new information and novel opportunities being developed at an astonishing pace across the entire globe, no one person can know or experience all that is necessary to thrive. And those who strive for really ambitious goals—who want to climb to the top of their chosen peaks—will find that partners are both more important and more difficult to find the higher they go.

As important as partners have been in my life, I could have made better use of them. I started to identify partners later than I might have—because after my childhood experiences, it took me some time to learn to trust people. Also, too often, I let partners choose me rather than actively seeking partners with the specific mix of skills and knowledge that I needed. You should begin as early as possible to consider the kind of friends, collaborators, and advisers you'll need around you, recognizing that those needs will evolve. Proactively reach out to the partners who will best serve your needs.

Our Prime Partners will have the most significant effect on our lives and the paths we travel. I have been extraordinarily lucky to have found the P1 of a lifetime. Barbara and I have been married for more than fifty years and have built a wonderful family around us. Through good times and tough times, our partnership has been sustained by qualities that I believe are essential for any successful P1 relationship: mutual love and respect, clear commitment, and willingness to make compromises and sacrifices. For P1s coming together today—in a culture frequently fixated on immediate gratification and not on the benefits of long-term connection—it is easy to overlook the imperative for commitment, compromise, and sacrifice.

In retrospect, I understand that my father's key passions and principles conflicted greatly with my mother's. They were an example—in this case a negative one—of how significantly your Prime Partner's passions and principles will affect your path and how far you go on it. The most successful P1s understand and accept their partner's passions and principles and are willing to compromise in pursuit of their own.

PLANS

Ultimately, the point of identifying your passions, principles, and partners is to choose a handful of priorities and use them to lay out a plan with concrete action steps. As the fable makes clear, a plan must be oriented to a specific context. I was lucky to learn early in life how to read my environment and assess my potential place in it. Today, the globalization of economics and culture make that reading and assessing both more difficult and more important than ever.

A plan is not simply a set of goals or destinations. It is not enough to say, "Now that I know who I am, I will climb that mountain over there." A plan describes a full journey, based on clear—sometimes difficult—choices. There is no perfect plan; striving for one will leave you frustrated.

And because a plan cannot be perfect, pursuing your plan demands the courage and willingness to explore alternatives when a particular path does not take you exactly where you anticipated it would. But there is a reward for that courage: even imperfect plans, if prepared thoughtfully and honestly, can lead us forward and enable us to climb our chosen peaks.

At the age of three, when my father kidnapped me, I began a long, uncertain journey. My destination was unclear and remained so for a long time. Ultimately, I came to understand that the only way to gain any sense of control over my life was to think ahead and plan. You and I are not so different in this respect. Our future path is veiled in a certain amount of darkness. As we make our way, we try to throw a little light onto it. We try to prepare for what we'll find.

The act of planning gives us some control over our fates. It helps us prepare for what luck brings our way. It increases the chances that our quests will be successful. If I've done my job right, *The Island of the Four Ps* will shed a little light on your path through the forest, enabling you to stride forward with a sense of confidence and optimism about the adventures before you. And it will help you achieve the four other Ps: perspective, purpose, pleasure, and peace.

Still, remember this: there is no universally right way to develop a plan. So I encourage you to apply my ideas (and your own) creatively, in the ways that work best for you. Allow my fable to spur your own stories, your own ways of thinking about the challenges facing your protagonists—especially the ultimate protagonist: you.

Each of us has "author rights" in our life stories. We can rewrite whatever story other people try to write for us. We can supply whatever ending we want to our stories—no matter how they started—and do our best to make it come to pass.

So grab your Tessamark and get planning.

ABOUT THE AUTHOR

ED HAJIM, the son of a Syrian immigrant, is a seasoned Wall Street executive with more than fifty years of investment experience. He has held senior management positions with the Capital Group, E. F. Hutton, and Lehman Brothers before becoming chairman and CEO of Furman Selz. Hajim has been the cochairman of ING Barings, Americas Region; chairman and CEO of ING Aeltus Group and ING Furman Selz Asset Management; and chairman and CEO of MLH Capital. In 2009, he became president of Diker Management and is now the nonexecutive chairman at HighVista Strategies. In 2008, after twenty years as a trustee of the University of Rochester, Hajim began an eight-year tenure as chairman of the university's board. Upon assuming that office he gave the school thirty million—the largest single donation in its history—to support scholarships and endow the Edmund A. Hajim School of Engineering and Applied Sciences. Through the Hajim Family Foundation, he has made generous donations to organizations that promote education, health care, arts, culture, and conservation. In 2015, he received the Horatio Alger Award, given to Americans who exemplify the values of initiative, leadership, and commitment to excellence and who have succeeded despite personal adversities. Hajim earned a BS in chemical engineering from the University of Rochester and an MBA with distinction from Harvard Business School. The father of three children and grandfather to eight, Hajim and his wife, Barbara, split their time between Key Largo, Florida, and Nantucket, Massachusetts.

VISIT THE AUTHOR AT EDHAJIM.COM.